TO
THE
BOTTOM
OF THE
SEA

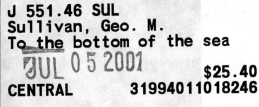

TO THE BOTTOM OF THE SEA

The Exploration of Exotic Life, the *Titanic*, and Other Secrets of the Oceans

GEORGE SULLIVAN

Twenty-First Century Books
Brookfield, Connecticut

The author is grateful to many individuals who provided background information for use in this book. Special thanks are due the following: Cindy L. Clark, Scripps Institution of Oceanography; Kathy Patterson, Woods Hole Oceanographic Institution; Michael Lorz and Judy Conrad, Columbus-America Discovery Group; Ellen J. Prager, U.S. Geological Survey; Corey Malcom, Mel Fisher Maritime Heritage Society; Susan J. Hanson, Harbor Branch Oceanographic Institution; Carla Wallace and Barbara Moore, National Oceanic and Atmospheric Administration; Barbara Muffler, Hawaii Undersea Research Laboratory; Mimi Dornack, National Geographic Society; Janice Aitchison, Lamont-Doherty Earth Observatory, Columbia University; Pat Clyne, Salvors, Inc., Key West, Florida; Lt. Christopher J. Madden and Henrietta Wright, Navy Office of Information; Maria Jacobson, Institute of Nautical Archaeology; Tom Hambright, Monroe County (Florida) Public Library; Wendy Tucker, Key West, Florida; and Dr. Richard Lutz, Rutgers University.

Cover photograph courtesy of The Institute of Nautical Archaeology

Photographs Courtesy of: Columbus-America Discovery Group: pp. 2-3, 58, 59; Woods Hole Oceanographic Institution: pp. 8, 17 (Tom Kleindinst), 22 (Albert Bradley), 49; Library Services, American Museum of Natural History: pp. 11 (C.H. Coles), 25, 30 (A. Rota); AP/Wide World Photos: pp. 13, 66, 70; Harbor Branch Oceanographic Institution: p. 28; U.S. Geological Survey: p. 32; Lamont-Doherty Earth Observatory (Bruce Heezen): p. 37; Hawaii Undersea Research Laboratory: pp. 40, 43; Institute of Nautical Archaeology: pp. 46, 48; Movie Star News: p. 62.

Library of Congress Cataloging-in-Publication Data
Sullivan, Geo. M. (George M.)
To the bottom of the sea: the exploration of exotic life, the Titanic, and other secrets of the oceans / George Sullivan.
p. cm.
Includes bibliographical references and index.
Summary: Examines different methods and technologies of undersea exploration, both past and present, the scientific discoveries that have been made, and the shipwrecks that have been explored.
ISBN 0-7613-0352-9 (lib. bdg.)
1. Underwater exploration—Juvenile literature. [1. Underwater exploration. 2. Shipwrecks.] I. Title.

GC65.S85   1999
551.46—dc21   98-41263   CIP   AC

Twenty-First Century Books
A Division of The Millbrook Press
2 Old New Milford Road
Brookfield, Connecticut 06804

CONTENTS

Exploring the Deep Sea 7

Alvin, *Argo*, and Beyond 15

Weird Life in the Deep Sea 24

Hot Water in the Cold Sea 33

Birth of an Island 39

Diving into History 45

Treasure Wreck 53

The *Titanic*: Discovery and Rediscovery 63

Source Notes 73

For More Information 76

Index 78

1

EXPLORING THE DEEP SEA

During the summer of 1986, Dr. Robert Ballard went where no living man or woman had ever gone before. Ballard, a marine geologist and explorer from Woods Hole Oceanographic Institution in Massachusetts, traveled 2.5 miles (4 kilometers) under the Atlantic Ocean to the wreck of the *Titanic*. The largest, most luxurious ocean liner in the world of its time, the *Titanic* sank in 1912, bringing death to 1,200 passengers.

Ballard did not go alone. He took with him an array of cameras to take still and video pictures from the undersea vessel *Alvin*. He also relied on a camera-robot named *Jason Junior*, which he launched from a "garage" at *Alvin*'s bow, to produce video coverage of the wreck. This marked the first time in nearly seventy-five years that parts of the *Titanic* would be viewed by humans.

Ballard's cameras showed that much of the *Titanic*'s hull was cloaked with thick rust. They recorded eerie pictures of deck railings and brass-rimmed portholes, and, at the ship's bow, the sturdy bitts used to secure mooring lines. Thousands

Carrying a three-person crew, the submersible Alvin *can dive to 15,000 feet (almost 2.5 miles or 4 kilometers), which gives it access to 86 percent of the world's ocean floor.*

of artifacts littered the ocean floor near the wreck, everything from wine bottles, copper cooking kettles, and cups and ashtrays to passenger suitcases and empty shoes.

Ballard called into question the theory that a long gash ripped into the *Titanic's* hull when the vessel struck an iceberg caused the ship to sink. Ballard found no long gash. Instead, he observed that the collision buckled seams in the hull, ripping out rivets, thereby flooding the great liner. "The damage was really separation of the plates" of the steel hull, said Ballard[1].

Ballard also recorded evidence that the ship had broken in two as it plunged beneath the sea. The stern section had settled on the ocean bottom almost 1,800 feet (550 meters) from the bow.

The finding of the *Titanic* triggered a wave of other expeditions to the bottom of the sea. In the late 1980s, through the 1990s and continuing into the new century, countless *submersibles* like *Alvin* began searching the darkness of the ocean's depths to discover huge deposits of mineral wealth, exotic sea creatures, strange geological formations, and tons of gold in deep-sea treasure wrecks.

A submersible is a thick-walled undersea vehicle, usually with a crew of two or three people, that can dive to great depths. Unlike a submarine, a submersible requires a support vessel to recharge its systems and house its crew.

This new era of exploration has also been aided by a number of remotely operated vehicles. These sophisticated robots, directed from research vessels at the surface, can collect samples of the sea bottom and send back video images of the terrain.

There's a great deal of exploring to do. The ocean covers nearly three-quarters of our planet's surface. It contains 97 percent of all the water on the planet and an enormous variety of living things. The ocean bottom has features as varied as those on land, including deep valleys, broad plains, and long mountain chains. Volcanoes on the seafloor vent steam and water into the underwater world.

Little was known of the ocean's depths until relatively recent times. Longtime myths and legends asserted that the deep ocean was populated with an assortment of fearsome serpents. Some scientists, shrugging off the tales of sea monsters, believed that the deep sea was a barren wasteland. Since it had no light and no nutrients, no life could survive there.

This theory was disproved during the 1800s when British scientists began to probe the dark regions of the ocean's depth. Some of their most notable discoveries resulted from a round-the-world expedition by a wooden sailing ship named the H.M.S. *Challenger* between 1872 and 1876. Using dredges and fishing nets, the *Challenger* hauled up thousands of animals from various depths. And from measurements of the water's depth taken by the *Challenger*'s crew, scientists were able to piece together a greater understanding of the physical makeup of the ocean bottom.

The *Challenger* was a surface vessel. Several decades were to pass before the introduction of a successful underwater vehicle that would allow scientists to travel to the ocean's depths themselves.

For centuries before the *Challenger*, humans had been experimenting with devices that would enable them to reach deep-sea waters. Humans, holding their breath, can't dive to much more than 30 to 40 feet (9 to 12 meters). At that depth, the water begins to exert painful pressure on the inner ear, sinuses, and lungs. And even the most efficient lungs can't hold a breath for more than a minute or so.

For thousands of years swimmers tried to figure out how to get oxygen underwater. Ancient Indian tribes in North America, when hunting ducks and other waterfowl, would conceal themselves underwater by drawing air through the stalks of hollow reeds.

The ancient Greeks lowered upside-down vases to divers. The air would stay trapped inside the vase until the diver sucked it out.

In the West Indies, the practice was to dip a small sponge in oil to trap the air inside, then dive, holding the sponge in one's mouth. Once beneath the surface, the diver would chew on the sponge to squeeze out the small amount of air it held.

Heavy and bulky helmeted, watertight diving suits, in which the person inside was linked by a hose to an air supply at the surface, first appeared in the 1800s. "Hard hat" diving gear, as it was called, remained in use well into the 1900s.

The word scuba is an acronym for *self-contained underwater breathing apparatus.* It consists of a portable underwater breathing system that is made up of a mouthpiece and valve joined by hoses strapped to the diver's back. Scuba is normally used at depths of as much as 100 feet (30 meters).

The technology of diving took a giant step forward in 1943 with the development of *scuba*. The invention of two Frenchmen, underwater explorer Jacques Cousteau and engineer Émile Gagnon, scuba enabled divers, breathing from tanks of compressed air strapped to their backs, to move freely underwater.

But even the most skilled and experienced scuba divers rarely dared to venture below 150 feet (46 meters). At such depths, too rapid a return from the high pressure of water to the lower atmospheric pressure at the surface is risky business. It can cause the release of nitrogen bubbles into the blood and tissues of a person's body, resulting in cramps, severe pain in the joints, and even death.

The world first began to get an idea of what might be possible in underwater exploration in 1930 when engineer Otis Barton, realizing that the sphere is the best shape to resist the tremendous pressures of the depths, invented the *bathysphere*.

During the early 1930s, William Beebe, a scientist and explorer working at the New York Zoological Society, made several dives in the bathysphere, once reaching a depth of more than half a mile off Bermuda. Peering through the bathysphere's

Cousteau, who died in 1997 at the age of eighty-seven, was fascinated by the sea throughout his life. His popular books, films, and television documentaries introduced the undersea world to millions.

The word *bathysphere* is formed from *bathy*, the Greek word for "deep," and *sphaira*, meaning "globe." The bathysphere was a metal diving ball with an interior diameter of 4.5 feet (1.4 meters) and walls 6 inches (15 centimeters) thick. Oxygen for breathing came from pressurized tanks. Lowered by a cable from a mother ship on the surface, William Beebe rode the bathysphere down more than half a mile. The bathysphere did not make any dives after 1934. It is on display today at the New York Aquarium at Coney Island in Brooklyn.

William Beebe's bathysphere, which dates from the 1930s, was the world's first research submarine.

6-inch (15-centimeter) circular window, Beebe looked out upon an undersea world populated by barely identifiable creatures that had never before been seen by humans, including exotic jellyfish and luminescent fish.[2]

In the 1940s, Auguste Piccard, a Swiss physicist, devised a manned vehicle to go much deeper. He called his invention a *bathyscaph*, from Greek words meaning "deep boat."

Instead of lowering the 7-foot (2-meter) steel ball that he had designed by means of a cable from a ship on the surface, as Beebe had done with his bathysphere, Piccard devised something different.

Earlier, Piccard had invented a high-altitude balloon that had taken him 9 miles (14.5 kilometers) above the earth, a feat that earned him the title of the world's highest flying human.[3] When he turned to conquering the depths of the sea, Piccard relied upon the same scientific principles that he had used in designing his stratosphere balloon.

In a balloon a gas, either helium or hydrogen, which are both lighter than air, lifts the balloon itself and the basket-shaped gondola beneath. In Piccard's underwater craft, a huge pontoon-shaped tank filled with gasoline, which is lighter than water, did the lifting necessary to bring the already lowered craft back to the surface. As in Beebe's bathysphere, pressurized tanks provided oxygen for breathing.

Piccard was ready to test his unusual craft in 1948. In waters just south of the Cape Verde Islands off Africa's west coast, the bathyscaph, with no men aboard, was sent down 4,600 feet (1,400 kilometers). Once the vehicle reached that level, tons of lead shotgun pellets carried by the bathyscaph to add weight and help it to sink, were released. The huge tank of gasoline then served to quickly lift the steel ball to the surface. The test was a success.

A tether is a cable, or the like, which links a submersible to a research vessel at the surface.

Piccard's craft was a big improvement over Beebe's bathysphere. Since it was not *tethered* to a support ship on the surface, the bathyscaph was not subject to the rough bumping around that the bathysphere sometimes endured when the mother ship moored in heavy seas. In addition, since there was no cable, Piccard's vehicle could rest comfortably on the ocean bottom.

In the years that followed the test dive, Piccard built an improved model of the bathyscaph. He named the craft *Trieste*, after the Italian city that had provided some of his financial support.

In 1953 the sixty-nine-year-old Piccard and his thirty-nine-year-old son, Jacques, in a test dive in the Mediterranean Sea off Naples, took the *Trieste* down almost 2 miles (3 kilometers). That feat and others captured the attention of scientists representing the U.S. Navy, who were eager to learn more about the depths of the seas. In 1958 the Office of Naval Research bought the *Trieste*, signed up Jacques Piccard as a consultant, and began development of an even more improved model of the bathyscaph.

In Auguste Piccard's bathyscaph Trieste, *the crew rode in a small steel sphere attached to a pontoon-shaped "balloon." The balloon held gasoline, which, being lighter than air, served to lift the sphere from the ocean's depths.*

An astonishing feat soon followed. Jacques Piccard and Lieutenant Don Walsh of the U.S. Navy took the new *Trieste* into the Challenger Deep (named for the research ship *Challenger*) early in 1960. The Challenger Deep is the deepest known spot in the undersea world. At the very bottom of the Mariana Trench, just east of the Marianas chain of islands in the western Pacific, the Challenger Deep reaches a depth of 35,840 feet (6.8 miles or 11 kilometers).

It took a total of nine hours for Piccard and Walsh to make the voyage to the bottom and return. Once the *Trieste* reached the seafloor, which Piccard and Walsh found to be covered with a light-colored ooze, strange creatures drifted past their porthole. One, as described by Piccard, was a "beautiful red shrimp." Another, an ivory-colored flatfish, had eyes in the side of its head.[4]

Trieste established the record for the deepest dive ever. And unless a deeper spot is discovered than that offered by the Challenger Deep, the *Trieste*'s record will stand for all time. It can be equaled but not exceeded.

Some U.S. Navy officials were fascinated by the new field of operations revealed by what the *Trieste* had accomplished. To continue investigations of the deep-sea world, the Navy drew up plans for a new type of underwater vehicle. The *Trieste* had no manipulator arms or grabbers, no collection baskets or sophisticated underwater cameras. The new craft would.

The unusual vessel would be big enough to hold three people and have the power to move on its own over the ocean bottom.

Charles B. Momsen, Jr., chief of Undersea Warfare at the Office of Naval Research, campaigned for the funds to build the new submersible. So did Allyn C. Vine, a scientist at the Woods Hole Oceanographic Institution. In Vine's honor, the craft was named *Alvin*. It was to write an important chapter in underwater discovery and research.

2

ALVIN, ARGO, AND BEYOND

"I think there's a perception that we have already explored the sea," says Sylvia Earle, a marine biologist and former chief scientist at the National Oceanographic and Atmospheric Administration. "The reality is we know more about Mars than we do about the oceans."[1]

That situation is in the midst of change. Thanks to a growing armada of thick-walled undersea vehicles, called submersibles, and more recently, an array of robot TV cameras and underwater *sonar* sleds, the vast mysteries of the deep sea are beginning to be solved.

The submersibles and robots are supported by a small fleet of multimillion-dollar research vessels. They boast precision navigation equipment and sophisticated satellite communications systems. Mounted at the stern of each is a sturdy A-frame crane that pivots forward to lower the submersible into the water, and pivots back to raise it.

Of all the submersibles at work today, none is more famous than *Alvin*. Built by the U.S. Navy in 1964, *Alvin* is operated by

Sonar, an acronym for *sound navigation and ranging*, is a system for detecting and locating submerged objects by listening with underwater microphones for sound waves that are reflected or produced by the objects.

the Woods Hole Oceanographic Institution. It is known officially as a deep submergence vehicle, or DSV.

The 28-foot (8.5-meter)-long *Alvin* carries a three-person crew made up of two scientists and a pilot. They are enclosed in a 7-foot (2-meter) passenger sphere. In a typical year, Alvin makes from 150 to 250 dives.

Today, *Alvin* is capable of descending to depths of almost 3 miles (5 kilometers). Most dives last from six to ten hours. When working at maximum depth, it takes almost two hours to reach the bottom and another two hours to get back to the surface.

When *Alvin* is lowered from its mother ship into the water, the submersible bobs up and down like a small boat. To dive, the pilot floods the main *ballast tanks* with water, which makes the vessel heavy and sends it to the bottom. To return to the surface, the pilot releases a set of heavy steel weights that are located on either side of the vessel. The lightened submersible then rises.

While on the bottom, *Alvin* pokes along, traveling at less than 2 miles (3 kilometers) an hour. Crew members peer through three small circular windows. One window looks forward; the others are at the sides. *Alvin* can also rest on the bottom or hover over a fixed point like a helicopter.

The hours spent on the sea bottom are crammed with carefully planned activity. Scientists record images of the undersea world using *Alvin*'s three video and two still cameras. *Alvin* carries twelve lights to illuminate the blackness of the deep ocean and make photography possible.

Using *Alvin*'s two highly maneuverable 6-foot (1.8-meter)-long arms, scientists collect geological samples or other types of specimens for study. Each arm is capable of lifting objects of suitcase size.

The 274-foot (84-meter) *Atlantis*, introduced in 1997, is one of the most advanced research vessels. *Atlantis* serves as *Alvin*'s mother ship.

Large, sometimes barrel-shaped containers carried by undersea vessels, ballast tanks contain water or other liquid (gasoline in the case of Piccard's bathyscaph), the amount of which is used to control the weight of the vessel, thus the depth at which the vehicle operates.

Sediment cores are compressed, cylinder-shaped samples of earth, rock, and organic material taken from the ocean floor for examination and study.

Inside Alvin's passenger sphere, the pilot looks out the front viewport. Scientists observe from either of two side viewports.

Instruments mounted at the front of the submersible enable scientists to sample water quality and temperature and remove *sediment cores* from the seafloor.

Despite all that *Alvin* has been able to accomplish, the world's first submersible was no overnight success. It took more than a decade after its construction before *Alvin* was accepted by the scientific community.

The vessel first gained widespread recognition in 1966, after a U.S. Air Force B-52 bomber was involved in a mid-air collision with another aircraft and dropped its cargo, a nuclear bomb, into the Mediterranean Sea off the coast of Spain. *Alvin* located the bomb and helped to bring it to the surface.

Still, few scientists were willing to choose *Alvin* for their work. They simply didn't trust the submersible. In its early years, *Alvin* often broke down. Scientists feared that *Alvin* might suddenly stop operating efficiently in the midst of a research project.

And *Alvin* was also shunned because the vessel was expensive to operate, costing about $25,000 a day.

In 1968 the situation got worse. During an unmanned dive, *Alvin* accidentally separated from its support cable and plunged to the ocean bottom almost a mile beneath the surface. It lay there lifeless for more than a year before it was raised by another submersible.

In the winter of 1972–1973, *Alvin* was dismantled and put back together with many new parts. Of all the improvements that were made, the most important involved the 7-foot (2-meter) personnel sphere that housed the three-person crew. It had originally been made of steel. In the "new" *Alvin*, the sphere was titanium, a lustrous white metal that is both lighter and much stronger than steel.

The titanium sphere more than doubled the depth at which *Alvin* could work. It was now possible for the vessel to endure the pressure at a depth of nearly 2.5 miles (4 kilometers).[2]

Before long, biologists and geologists were lining up for a chance to use *Alvin*. Physicists, engineers, and marine chemists wanted to dive, too.

In the years that followed the introduction of *Alvin*, many other submersibles were built. Among them were *Turtle* and *Sea Cliff*, a pair of American submersibles that resemble *Alvin* in appearance. *Turtle* is capable of operating at depths of close to 2 miles (3 kilometers), while *Sea Cliff* can operate as deep as 4 miles (6 kilometers) below the surface.

The fleet also came to include a French submersible named *Nautile*, an advanced version of *Alvin*. *Nautile* is named after the nautilus, a spiral-shelled mollusk that lives in the Indian and Pacific oceans. The nautilus uses its spiral shell to rise and fall through the ocean waters.

Bright yellow in color, *Nautile* is 25 feet (8 meters) in length and 6 feet (1.8 meters) in diameter at its widest point. It can descend to a depth of more than 3 miles (5 kilometers). There is room inside for three people. Each passenger has a porthole.

One crew member sits before two pairs of 8-inch (20-centimeter) television screens. Two of these monitors are linked to a pair of video cameras. The two other monitors are connected to cameras that focus on *Nautile*'s mechanical arms.

Nautile operates from the mother ship *Nadir*. (In both French and English, nadir means "lowest point.")

Russia has built twin submersibles, the *Mir I* and *Mir II*, which can dive to depths of nearly 4 miles (6 kilometers). They have completed a variety of important assignments. In 1995 they were used in producing stunning views of the *Titanic*.

In 1990 the Japanese introduced the *Shinkai 6500*, which cost about $60 million to build. With the ability to carry its three-person crew to a depth of more than 4 miles, the *Shinkai 6500* has earned acclaim as the world's deepest-diving submersible.[3]

One of the biggest disadvantages of *Shinkai 6500*, *Nautile*, *Mir I*, *Mir II*, *Alvin*, and other such submersibles is that they can stay underwater for only a relatively short time, from six to ten hours. They then must return to the surface to have their batteries recharged.

Fresh batteries are vital to a submersible. The batteries keep running a fan that pumps the vessel's air through a canister filled with sodium hydroxide. This system acts as a "scrubber" that removes carbon dioxide given off by crew members as they breathe. Were the air not cleansed, the submersible's passengers would be poisoned by their own exhalations.

This problem of having only a limited amount of time on the ocean bottom has been solved in part through the introduction of robot TV cameras and underwater sonar sleds that were developed during the mid-1980s by the Woods Hole Oceanographic Institution's Deep Submergence Laboratory.

Dr. Robert Ballard used one such device, *Argo*, in his discovery of the *Titanic* in 1985. A remotely operated sonar sled that is 15 feet (4.6 meters) in length, *Argo* is lowered on a tether to within 50 feet (15 meters) of the sea bottom. The sled produces detailed images of as much as an acre of the seafloor at a time, a vast improvement over what was previously possible.

The tether that links *Argo* to the research ship is a steel-armored cable that is only two-thirds of an inch in diameter. Despite its slimness, the tether is capable of supporting a weight of 35,000 pounds (15,876 kilograms).[4]

Argo's advanced sonar system develops a clear picture of the ocean bottom, including such features as canyons and mountain ranges. During 1986, the year that followed *Argo's* discovery of the *Titanic*, the robot was used in mapping the East Pacific Rise off Mexico, an area of active volcanoes. *Argo's* sonar found many new hot springs and sites of recent volcanic eruptions.

Argo does not normally investigate the deep sea all by itself. It was designed to work with a camera-carrying robot named *Jason*. Just as *Argo* is tethered to a large research vessel at the surface, so *Jason* is tethered to *Argo*.

Jason is about 7 feet (2 meters) long and equipped with lights and cameras. It was developed in the late 1980s at Woods Hole.

In 1986, *Jason Junior*, an early version of the craft, was used in videotaping the *Titanic*. It threaded its way through the *Titanic's* passageways, ascended its staircases, and entered its ballrooms to send back stunning pictures of the wrecked ship.

They called it "mowing the lawn." It's the term that deep-sea searchers used to describe their method for finding something on the ocean floor that they were trying to recover. It could have been a lost treasure ship, a downed airplane, or a bomb or missile that got away.

A research ship dragged a weighted sonar-equipped device, sometimes called a tow fish, back and forth over the search area. The tether that linked the tow fish to the vessel at the surface could be several miles long, which made it difficult to work with any precision.

It was boring, too. The ship usually had to travel at less than 1 knot (the equivalent of about 1.15 miles, or 1.85 kilometers) per hour.[5] This meant that the search could take weeks or months or even years. Mel Fisher, the most noted of all treasure seekers, "mowed the lawn" in the Gulf of Mexico for some sixteen years before finding the Spanish galleon *Atocha,* which was laden with gold and silver worth several hundred million dollars.

The fact that the surface vessel had to move at a snail's pace was only part of the problem. When the sonar did register a "hit"—that is, reported something interesting—the whole process had to come to a halt. The tow fish was reeled in, and a remotely operated camera system was lowered to the site. If the camera confirmed that something worthwhile had been spotted, the object was investigated. If not, the camera was recovered, the tow fish lowered, and the searchers started "mowing the lawn" again.

Now there is a better way to do the job. It involves the use of a new generation of undersea craft—torpedolike robots that can be programmed to prowl miles beneath the surface, then go in close and investigate when something interesting has been discovered. Underwater research that used to require days or weeks of work can now be completed in hours.

Such robots are known as AUVs—autonomous underwater vehicles. An AUV has no tether. It is battery powered and loaded with computer chips. Once it is programmed, a ship or aircraft drops off the robot, then returns to pick it up days or months later.

An AUV is capable of remaining on the ocean bottom for as long as a year while accumulating pictures and data.

The U.S. Navy began development work on such robots in the early 1970s. The first successful model was 17 feet (5 meters) long and weighed 2,800 pounds (1,270 kilograms), and shaped like a torpedo. It was completed in 1984.[6]

The robot could automatically go from "mowing the lawn" to inspecting a target up close. Then it would go back to wide area searching. When the search was completed, the robot dropped the weights it carried and rose to the surface to be recovered.

Out of this development work came ABE (autonomous benthic explorer), a tetherless, unmanned undersea robot that is operated by the Woods Hole Oceanographic Institution. ABE carried out its first scientific mission in 1995.

The torpedo-shaped ABE, for autonomous benthic explorer, is a robot that can remain underwater for as long as a year at a time, recording images and collecting environmental information.

Once placed in the water, ABE descends to the ocean floor where it collects environmental information, makes videos, and snaps still photographs. The robot is designed to operate at a depth of 12,000 to 18,000 feet (3,658 to 5,486 meters).

ABE is programmed to "sleep" most of the time so as to conserve the life of its batteries. But once a day the robot awakens and moves about over a preplanned course to carry out its assigned chores. ABE's first missions involved the investigation of *hydrothermal vents* and ocean dump sites.

A hydrothermal vent is an opening in the ocean floor that spews hot gases and volcanic material from beneath the earth's crust.

It's not likely that ABE and other robots that can operate without human guidance are going to replace the great multitude of research vehicles that includes *Alvin, Nautile, Argo, Jason,* and so many others. But AUVs are sure to be part of the mix.

The ways in which this vast fleet of vehicles is being used are even more varied than the vehicles themselves. While the discovery and investigation of the *Titanic* is perhaps the most noted of their accomplishments, such vehicles are also being employed on a wide range of other scientific missions, including a search for the many forms of exotic creatures that inhabit the deep sea.

3

WEIRD LIFE IN THE DEEP SEA

It was almost like finding a tyrannosaur in a supermarket parking lot. In 1938 scientists that specialize in the study of fossils were astounded to learn that fishermen off the coast of South Africa had pulled up a coelacanth (pronounced *sea*-la-canth, a strange fishlike creature about 5 feet (1.5 meters) long, blue in color, with strange fins below its body that were somewhat like human legs in appearance.

The coelacanth was thought to have died out shortly after the end of the Mesozoic era, the age of dinosaurs. The fishermen's find won worldwide attention as a "living fossil."

Today, thanks to deep-diving submersibles and video cameras mounted on remotely operated undersea vehicles, many rare species of fish such as the coelacanth are no longer a mystery. The coelacanth, in fact, has been the subject of study by Dr. Hans Fricke and other scientists of Germany's Max Planck Institute for Behavioral Physiology.

Many of the fish and other creatures known to inhabit the deep ocean are very strange. Some have the ability to create

Once believed to be extinct, the coelacanth is now the subject of intense study. This is a model of the fish.

light to lure unsuspecting prey or frighten away predators. Many have a snakelike appearance. One, the gulper eel, can stretch its jaws to devour prey larger than itself.

The coelacanth has its own set of distinctive traits. Dr. Fricke and his fellow scientists have discovered concentrations of coelacanths living off the coast of Grand Comore, the largest of the islands that make up the Federal Islamic Republic of Comoros. The islands are in the Indian Ocean, strewn between the northern tip of the island of Madagascar and the African coast.[1]

Dr. Fricke believes that about two hundred coelacanths live in a 5-mile (8-kilometer) stretch off the Grand Comore coast. He and his colleagues have descended in a submersible provided by the German government to study them.

The coelacanths live in underwater caves at a depth of about 650 feet (198 meters). They hunt at night, ranging to the sea bottom for their prey. They rest in the caves during the day.

Dr. Fricke and other scientists are concerned that one day soon the coelacanth may become extinct. While the coelacanth has no commercial value itself, it lives in an area that is heavily fished by Comorians for other species of fish. Coelacanths sometimes grab the bait and hooks meant for other fish, and are pulled to the surface.

Few survive very long. The fish are almost always seriously injured by fishhooks. Bringing the fish to the surface from its deep-ocean habitat is also very harmful.

Their fearful appearance also works against them. Since coelacanths have powerful jaws that are lined with razor-sharp teeth, fishermen often club them to avoid being bitten.

Various government agencies have sought to prevent commercial fishermen from fishing in areas where the coelacanth lives. One strategy was to anchor "fish attractors" in waters farther from shore than the coelacanth is known to inhabit. The attractors were long, narrow strips of brightly colored plastic.

The plan worked, at least in part. The streamers did attract most of the ordinary fish, and not the coelacanths. But the streamers were anchored so far from shore that the fishermen were reluctant to paddle their canoes to the specified area. They preferred working closer to shore. The fish attractors were removed, and the fish returned to the coelacanth zone. The number of coelacanths continued to diminish as a result.[2]

Coelacanths are members of a very ancient order of "fringe finned" fish. They have fins below their bodies that are somewhat similar to legs both in shape and in movement. For this reason, some scientists believe that coelacanths are closely related to the line of fishes that gave rise to the first vertebrate to walk on land. This means that the ancestors of the coelacanths swimming off Grand Comore Island may well be the ancestors of human beings.

As Dr. Fricke has pointed out, the coelacanth is "something special." He says, "It is a remarkable fish, a window into the distant past, and a treasure of nature. If we let him die out, it will be a tragedy."[3]

Unlike the coelacanth, which is several feet in length, most deep-sea fish are smaller than those that inhabit shallow water. During a thirty-day mission off the southern coast of Cuba in 1998, American and Cuban biologists sought to capture one such specimen, a rare member of the goby family. The fish was only 8 inches (20 centimeters) long and weighed a mere 4 ounces (113 grams).[4]

The expedition was headed by Grant Gilmore of the Harbor Branch Oceanographic Institute near Fort Pierce on Florida's east coast and conducted from within the *Johnson Sea Link*, a four-person submersible that is capable of capturing live fish and returning with them to the surface.

The *Sea Link* became famous in 1986 when it found the crew cabin of the space shuttle *Challenger*, which had exploded after being launched from Cape Kennedy, Florida.

During the expedition, the scientists made some fifty dives in the *Sea Link*, each lasting three to four hours. Their goal was to snare one of the goby fish in a 2- by 3-foot (0.6- by 0.9-meter) trap. While they sighted the fish several times, they were unable to capture one.

One morning, their luck changed. "It was a thirty-minute cat-and-mouse game with the fish," said Gilmore. When the fish drifted above the *Sea Link*, the pilot pointed the submersible straight up. A crew member opened the trap. When the fish disappeared from view, the scientists knew that it had been sucked into the trap. "More than 2,000 feet [610 meters] below the water's surface there was screaming and yelling and celebrating like you never heard before," Gilmore recalled.[5]

The expedition was notable because it marked the first time that an American research vessel had been permitted to enter Cuban waters since Cuba's leader Fidel Castro came to power in 1959. The team explored nearly 700 miles (1,127 kilometers) of Cuba's southern coast.

The scientists were amazed at the richness of the waters as compared with the ocean off the coast of Florida, which has become polluted. Gilmore described the southern coast of Cuba as being "like what Florida may have been years ago." He said that he and the other scientists had seen "hundreds of times" more fish and lobsters than could be presently seen in Florida Bay or the Florida Keys.

Harbor Branch Oceanographic Institution's four-person submersible Johnson Sea Link can dive to depths of as much as 3,000 feet (914 meters).

While scientists have made significant progress in finding unusual new types of underwater life, one well-known inhabitant of the deep remains a mystery, the giant squid. The subject of more horror stories than Frankenstein's monster, the giant squid has yet to be seen alive in its natural habitat.[6]

It's not that scientists haven't tried. Using submersibles and robot vehicles with their powerful lights and cameras, biologists and oceanographers have made countless attempts to capture a giant squid, but without success.

Fishermen, by accident, occasionally land one of the giants in their nets or trawls. But in such cases the animal has usually been terribly battered or even hacked to pieces, and is scarcely recognizable.

Squids are cephalopods, close relatives of octopuses and cuttlefish, and distant cousins of clams and oysters. Their long, shimmering bodies have rear fins. Their eyes, as complex as those of humans, are sometimes the size of dinner plates. These are the largest eyes in the animal kingdom.[7]

The squid has ten arms, eight of which are short and thick. The two others, called tentacles, are longer and thinner. The ends of the tentacles are covered with many circular suckers.

There are scores of species of squids. While the giant squid is known to be as much as 60 feet (18 meters) in length, as long as a school bus, there are types that are smaller than a cricket.

Many squids have light organs that adorn their long bodies. Their colors can include sky blue, ruby red, and snow white. Squids can switch from one color to another in the blink of an eye. This quality helps squids to elude the sea life that preys upon them. Squids are the chief form of food of the sperm whale.

Some species of squids have the ability to shoot an inky liquid into the water when seeking to escape a predator. One scientist calls the ink a "pseudomorph." This means that the ink is supposed to resemble the body of a squid so as to fool the predator into attacking the ink rather than its escaping quarry. For example, a long, thin squid ejects a long, slim patch of ink. A short, round squid ejects an ink field that is short and round.

The giant squid has never been seen, and no photographs of it are known to exist. Here a model of the giant creature hovers above display cases at the American Museum of Natural History in New York City.

Through the centuries, the giant squid has been characterized as one of the most fearsome of sea monsters. Its encircling arms were described as being long and powerful enough to crush the biggest of sailing ships.

In his book *20,000 Leagues Under the Sea*, published in 1870, Jules Verne described the giant squid in frightening detail. He reported that it lived in deep caverns in the sides of undersea cliffs. The openings to the caves were shrouded in masses of tangled weeds.

As Captain Nemo, the main character of the book, and his submarine *Nautilus* ranged close to one of these dark, forbidding caverns, a passenger saw a "formidable, swarming, wriggling movement." Captain Nemo and his gallant crew were soon battling a horde of giant squids and their overwhelming arms and tentacles. Early sailors trembled at the thought of such an encounter.

Such fears have endured. "I have a lot of respect for these animals," said Dr. Ellen C. Forch, a New Zealand biologist who studied the giant squid for more than fifteen years. While Dr. Forch was curious to learn as much as possible about the creature, she had no plans to descend to its habitat, more than half a mile below the surface, in a tiny submersible. Dr. Forch preferred to study the giant squid from a surface vessel. "I have small children," she said, "and they need their mother."[8]

Dr. Forch is one of a number of New Zealand scientists who have been diligently studying the giant squid. They have been joined by Dr. Clyde Roper, curator of mollusks and a squid expert at the National Museum of Natural History at the Smithsonian Institution in Washington, D.C.

Their work has also been concerned with smaller squid that live in the sea's middle waters. "We've seen them doing all kinds of things that we thought they couldn't do," said Dr. Roper.[9] For example, squids were once believed to be slow and sluggish, drifting about with their tentacles held straight out. But scientists have observed them moving briskly, even doing flips and cartwheels. "We have to re-think the animal," said one scientist.

In gathering material for a television program called "Sea Monsters: Search for the Giant Squid," Dr. Roper traveled to the South Pacific near New Zealand, entered the *Johnson Sea Link*, the submersible operated by the Harbor Branch Oceanographic Institution, and descended to the ocean's depths. His goal was to capture video images of the giant squid, if not the animal itself.

While Dr. Roper was able to discover new facts about the creature and its environment, he was unable to film the elusive squid. Despite his many setbacks, Dr. Roper has no doubt that one day soon somebody will actually see a giant squid and record its image. Until then, capturing the giant squid remains one of the great challenges of natural history and undersea photography.

The giant squid, tiny members of the goby family, and exotic coelacanths represent only a small portion of the strange forms of life that are being revealed to scientists probing the deep sea. Vast communities of little-known creatures have been discovered at the ocean's bottom wherever heat from the earth's core is being released into the water. It's a bizarre world of life without light.

Tube worms extend their fragile tentacles into the water in search of passing food. These particular tube worms are known as Christmas tree worms.

4

HOT WATER IN THE COLD SEA

The seafloor offers features that are just as varied as those found on dry land. Vast flat stretches of it are similar to the plains areas of the American Midwest. Tall mountain chains jut up from the ocean bottom, and deep valleys cut into it.

In the late 1970s off the Galápagos Islands in the eastern Pacific Ocean, scientists discovered a mysterious feature—cracks in the ocean floor from which hot water spouted. Heat from the earth's core was being released into the water.

As scientists continued to study these hydrothermal vents, they saw that the hot water supported vast communities of strange marine life. These included clams the size of dinner plates, huge mussels, and clusters of white crabs.

Other creatures of the vents were even more exotic. There were colonies of worms, some 8 feet (2.4 meters) long, that stood upright, swaying back and forth in the ocean currents. Called tube worms, they looked like something from another planet.

There seemed to be no food supply. All living things depend on plants for food, and plants require the energy they get from sunlight for photosynthesis, the process by which they make food. No living thing, scientists believed, could survive without light.

But for the tube worms, mussels, and clams that populated the undersea vent fields, where the sun's rays never penetrate, light and photosynthesis weren't necessary. Instead, they lived off the masses of microbes that fed upon the sulfurous compounds thrown off by the hot vents. This process is called chemosynthesis.

Scientists who have studied hydrothermal vents say that the microbes they produce may be very much like the first forms of life on Earth. They date from a time many millions of years ago when the planet had the harsh type of environment now found in the oceans' depths.

Scientists later discovered bizarre-looking crabs and shrimp, and hundreds of other types of living organisms in hydrothermal vent fields. At the Galápagos vent site, scientists sighted an unusual pink, blue-eyed fish. "It was the only fish we knew of that loved being in the vent water," said biologist Bob Hessler, "as opposed to being nearby."[1]

The scientists wanted to capture one of the fish to study it. On a return trip to the Galápagos in 1979, they failed in their attempts to net one. In 1985 they failed again.

In 1988, aboard the submersible *Alvin*, dozens of the fish were sighted. Using a net in one of *Alvin*'s manipulator claws, biologist Ralph Hollis snagged one of the fish on the first swing of the net. He was so excited that he dropped the net. "I had my heart in my mouth because I wanted it so badly," Hollis said.[2] But Hollis managed to recover both the net and the fish, and the submersible returned to the surface with it.

Later, at a shore laboratory, the geologists studied the fish. They found the creature to be a new species. But they were unable to determine why the fish lived in such a peculiar place as a vent field. The warm water there was high in hydrogen sulfide, but low in oxygen.

The water spewing from hydrothermal vents also contains such minerals as copper and zinc, as well as sulfur compounds. As the scalding water comes in contact with the colder sea, the minerals settle out and form deposits around the vents.

These deposits often take on a chimneylike appearance through which the murky clouds of water and gases continue to escape. To scientists peering out at this activity, it looks like black smoke is gushing from a formation that resembles a factory chimney. They have nicknamed these hot vents "black smokers."

The world's largest black smoker, located in the Pacific Ocean on the northernmost section of the Juan de Fuca Ridge off the coast of Oregon, is about the same size as a 16-story building. That chimney is called Godzilla.

Godzilla is so big that scientists have never seen the whole thing at one time. In a submersible such as *Alvin*, the searchlights are capable of illuminating only about 50 feet (15 meters) of the deep-ocean darkness. Because Godzilla is 160 feet (49 meters) in height, scientists see only about one-third of the structure at a time.

Since the discovery of hydrothermal vents in the late 1970s, scientists around the globe have pinpointed more than fifty other sites along mid-ocean ridges, in depths of 8,200 to 10,000 feet (2,500 to 3,048 meters), where the strange formations occur. Scientists have forecast that hundreds more will be found.

To a growing army of scientists, hydrothermal vents provide excitement, not only because of the strange creatures they sustain but also because of concentrations of rare minerals they include. In 1980 and 1981, a team of explorers and geochemists, using *Alvin*, visited the Galápagos vent field off the coast of South America where deep-sea hot springs had first been discovered. Almost by accident, the team came upon a huge concentration of metallic ores, estimated to be half a mile in length, 650 feet (198 meters) wide, and 130 feet (40 meters) thick.

If the ore could be mined commercially, it would be worth a fortune. Iron, zinc, magnesium, aluminum, lead, nickel, mercury, copper, tungsten, and silver were present at the site. The copper alone was judged to be worth $2 billion.

The Gorda Ridge, about 70 miles (113 kilometers) off the Oregon and northern California coasts, was hailed as another undersea site that offered enormous potential for its mineral riches. It was vast, believed to include an area the size of the state of New York.

The mineral treasures of the Gorda Ridge excited the federal government. This was during the early 1980s, when the United States and the Soviet Union were in the midst of the Cold War, a period of intense political and military rivalry between the two nations.

The Gorda Ridge was seen as a source of vital material for making weapons and military hardware. Secretary of the Navy John Lehman said, "Of the nearly two dozen strategic minerals on which America is now wholly dependent on overseas sources," nearly all "could be provided from the sea bottom."[3]

But nothing ever came of the plans to mine the rich deposits of the seabed. Industry officials showed no interest in the task, saying that it was too expensive and too risky.

It was also controversial. Environmentalists said that mining the deep-sea vent sites would pollute and destroy the ecosystem of the hot springs.

There was nothing new about plans to mine the seabed. During the 1950s and 1960s, scientists of many nations were aware that concentrations of manganese nodules littered the seabed. They were not certain just how these potatolike lumps had formed. They did know, however, that there were trillions of them.

Some of the most valuable accumulations of these nodules were to be found at a depth of a mile or so in the Pacific Ocean east of Hawaii. There the lumpy deposits were spread over thousands of miles of seabed.

Upon examination, the nodules appeared to be made up of a long list of rare metals and thus were a source of great riches. They were composed of as much as 25 percent manganese, a hard, grayish white metal, which was used in strengthening steel. Manganese is also used in making bulldozer teeth and the armor plating in battle tanks. The lumps also contained small amounts of cobalt, nickel, and copper, all highly valued by American industry.

But the plans to recover this mineral wealth were shelved. Mines on land, it was found, had plentiful deposits of manganese and the other mineral compounds. It

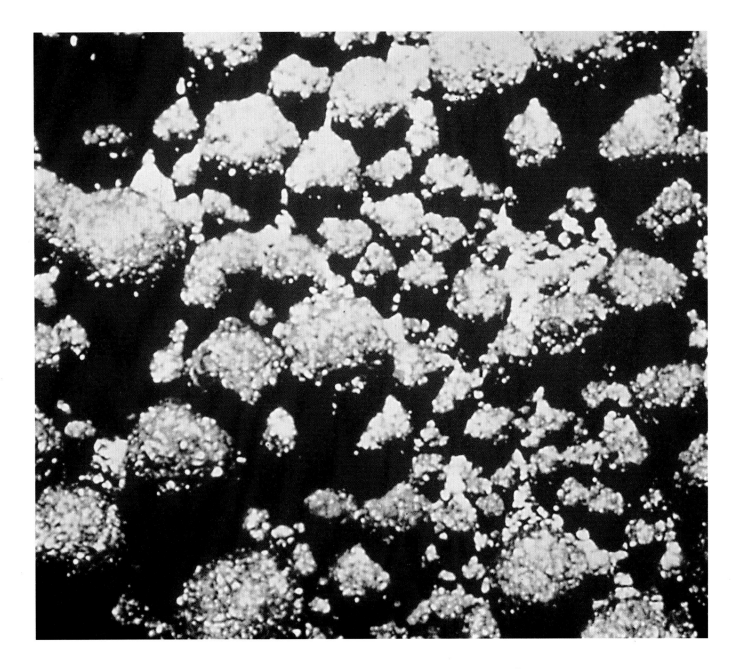

*Manganese nodules on the
seafloor south of Australia*

was cheaper to mine the land supplies than to try to scrape the metal nodules from the sea bottom.

Another plan for mining was unveiled late in 1997 when Australian businessmen and scientists staked a claim to much larger and richer undersea deposits of gold, silver, and copper in the South Pacific. The site covers nearly 2,000 square miles (5,180 square kilometers)—an area about the size of the state of Delaware—of the territorial waters of Papua New Guinea.

In this part of the world, the seabed is alive with hydrothermal vents. The chimneys and other rocky shapes that have formed are rich in a wide range of metal compounds, including gold, silver, copper, iron, and zinc. It amounts to billions of dollars in metal ores.[4]

The metal-rich deposits were discovered in 1991 and 1993 by Dr. Ray Binns, an Australian scientist, and Dr. Steven D. Scott, a marine geologist at the University of Toronto. "The gold content is incredibly high," said Dr. Scott. It is the "most gold," he said, ever found to occur naturally in the deep sea.[5]

If the mineral concentrations turn out to be as valuable as indicated, the company plans to start mining early in the twenty-first century.

DSVs such as *Alvin* and *Nautile*, remotely operated sonar sleds, and camera-equipped robot vehicles are expected to be enlisted in pinpointing the location of the deposits.

Giant claws lowered from surface ships will do the mining, and this has given rise to environmental concerns. Scientists worry about significant damage to surrounding plant and animal life. "Great care should be taken," says Dr. Sylvia A. Earle, a marine biologist and former chief scientist of the National Oceanic and Atmospheric Administration.

Dr. Earle and other environmentally concerned scientists have argued that a significant portion of the New Guinea site should be made a "no take" zone—that is, off limits to mining. In that way, rare seabed species could be preserved, and scientists would have an opportunity to study the hot springs, black smokers, and the various forms of bacterial life that they support.

5

BIRTH
OF AN
ISLAND

In 1990 geologist Alexander Malahoff teamed with Russian scientists, and using one of Russia's *Mir* submersibles, began diving to investigate the hot chimneys and other formations near the Loihi undersea volcano, about 15 miles (24 kilometers) southeast of the big island of Hawaii.

The volcano's summit was slightly more than a half-mile below the water's surface. Its sides dropped almost straight down to the floor of the ocean, some 9,000 feet (2,743 meters) below.

In the first years that Malahoff studied Loihi (which means "long, tall one" in Hawaiian), the volcano was quiet. Said Malahoff, who had become director of the National Oceanic and Atmospheric Administration's Hawaii Undersea Research Laboratory, "We thought it was a gentle volcano."

Then in July 1996, seismometers, detecting devices that receive evidence of the earth's vibrations, began to register a series of violent tremors from Loihi. Fred Duennebier, a seismologist at the University of Hawaii, suspected that Loihi was

This underwater seismometer helped to measure earthquake activity at Loihi.

erupting. Duennebier realized that he and his colleagues were being presented with an unusual opportunity. They could be the first scientists to witness the violence of an undersea volcano.

Duennebier and other scientists reached an area in the waters above Loihi in the research vessel *Ka'imikai o Kanaloa* in early August 1996. One of the first things they did was to lower underwater microphones, called sonobuoys, into the water. As the *K o K* cruised back and forth over the volcano, the radio receivers aboard the research ship rang out with a steady stream of cracks, crashes, and booms. "It was very nerve wracking," said one of the scientists. "It sounded like hell was breaking loose underneath the ship."[1]

It didn't take long for the sonar impulses that were mapping the site to reveal that something strange had happened. In the years that the scientists had been diving to study Loihi, they had established that the volcano's summit enclosed an area of active hydrothermal vents that was about the size of a football field. They called the area "Pele's Vents," after the Hawaiian goddess of volcanoes.

But on the K o K's sonar imaging, neither the summit nor the vents could be seen. Instead of a broad expanse of vents and chimneys spouting gases and molten rock, there was a big hole. It was as if Loihi's summit had disappeared.

Seismologist Duennebier refused to believe what the sonar was reporting. "Look, we've just made a mistake in navigation," he said. "We'll cross the summit again.

"So we did, and it was still gone. And we crossed it again, and it was still gone. It was a real shocker."[2]

The next day, with the earthquake activity dwindling, Duennebier and the other scientists decided it was safe enough to launch Pisces V, a three-person submersible, with the ability to perform many of the same tasks as Alvin.

Duennebier dove with geologist Frank Sansone and the pilot of the submersible, Terry Kerby. After a descent that lasted about a half-hour, Pisces V approached the area where Loihi's summit and vents gushing hydrothermal fluids had once been clearly seen.

As they looked through the submersible's tiny windows, the three scientists found themselves peering over the edge of a cliff into a cavernous hole. As one of the scientists later remarked, "It was as if fifty million dump trucks full of lava had gone someplace."

The research team was surprised that such an enormous collapse had not triggered a giant tsunami, a tidal wave. Such a huge, towering wall of water could have been powerful enough to destroy Waikiki, the resort district of Honolulu within seconds, according to Malahoff. Apparently the collapse of the summit had taken place over several days, not in an instant, which served to drain the great mass of water of its destructive power.

The scientists established that the newly created hole measured almost a half-mile across and nearly 1,000 feet (305 meters) in depth. They dubbed it "Pele's Pit."

In the months that followed, researchers boarded *Pisces V* and descended into Pele's Pit a dozen times. Awesome sights greeted them at the bottom of the new crater.

Slowly, *Pisces V* picked its way past great towers of lava and cliff faces that were several hundred feet in height. There were teetering boulders the size of buses. When the submersible accidentally brushed a huge rock, the research team heard the scary rumble of landslides behind them. The pilot quickly steered toward the middle of the pit for safety.

Although Pele's Vents had disappeared, everywhere the scientists looked they saw new vents, some 20 feet (6 meters) across. From the vents a mixture of super-heated water and dissolved minerals spurted from the earth's core.

The vents also nourished churning clouds of bacteria. So thick were the free-flowing swarms of bacteria that they limited visibility to only a few feet as the three men sought to look out of the submersible's windows. The bacteria occupied every surface around the vents, sometimes forming into thick mats.

"There was slime everywhere," said Malahoff. The regions around the hydro-thermal vents, Malahoff noted, were thick with bacterial communities spread in sheets and clumps. The scene reminded him of clustered cobwebs in a haunted house.[3]

The bacteria grew fast. Frank Sansone and other scientists aboard *Pisces V*, wielding a suction device with a submersible claw, vacuumed up samples of the bacteria, leaving an 8-inch (20-centimeter) hole in one of the mats. When they returned to the site two days later, the scientists were surprised to see that new bacteria had formed, filling the hole in the mat. "It was as if we had never been there," said Sansone.

The mats are usually white or tan in color, according to Sansone. When sections were peeled from the ocean floor and brought back to the laboratory, the mats, and the water in which they were collected, reeked of sulfur. And on close examination,

To document the day-to-day changes in the new vent field at Loihi, scientists planted this Ocean Bottom Observatory on the seafloor.

the scientists found that the microbe mats were loaded with heavy metals and toxic compounds from the volcano. "If this site were a factory, it would be heavily regulated by the Environmental Protection Agency," Sansone joked.[4]

The research team was not sure of the exact sequence of events that occurred during the summer of 1996 that caused the collapse of Loihi's summit and the creation of the huge, vent-filled crater. But Malahoff said it was the same process by which the volcanic Hawaiian chain of islands was formed.

The molten rock had burst through the earth's crust. In so doing, it triggered the earthquakes that the scientific team had recorded, and caused the collapse of the rock dome that had formed Loihi's summit.

The volcano will eventually build mountains high enough to jut through the surface of the ocean. But that mountain-making process will take fifty thousand years or so.

All that is happening continues to be monitored by scientists representing the Hawaii Undersea Research Laboratory. They are watching and listening as a volcano at the bottom of the Pacific Ocean seeks to create another island in the Hawaiian chain.

6

DIVING INTO HISTORY

In the summer of 1984, about a year before Robert Ballard and his colleagues from the Woods Hole Oceanographic Institution discovered the *Titanic*, another team of scientists, operating in the eastern Mediterranean Sea off the coast of Turkey, began probing the remains of what they believed might be the world's oldest shipwreck.

The wreck had been discovered two years earlier by a Turkish sponge diver off Uluburun, near the Turkish resort town of Kas. It dated from about 1316 B.C.

It was unusual not merely because of its age. Once a richly laden trading vessel, the 3,300-year-old Uluburun Wreck contained artifacts that represented a great assortment of ancient cultures—Greek, Cypriot, Kassite, Old Babylonian, Assyrian, Canaanite, Baltic, Egyptian, and Mycenaean. "An archaeologist's dream," one scientist called it.

The principal items carried by the ship included copper *ingots* weighing about 60 pounds (27 kilograms) apiece. There were also many large storage jars, called amphoras. The jars

An ingot is a mass of metal, in this case copper, that is roughly shaped into a usable form for storage or transportation, and which will be processed and used for something else later.

Scuba-equipped archaeologists probe the remains of the ancient shipwreck in the Mediterranean Sea off the coast of Uluburun, Turkey. In the foreground is an ancient stone anchor.

held several different types of cargo, including glass beads and *resin*. Gold, silver, ivory, ebony, and ostrich eggs were also aboard.[1]

A solid-gold good-luck piece, or amulet, in the shape of a beetle was one of the most curious items recovered. It bore the name of Queen Nefertiti of Egypt.[2] The amulet was found in the midst of a collection of scrap gold. To archaeologists, this indicated that it was an object that may have been pawned or lost. If the ship had reached its destination, the gold beetle probably would have been melted down.

The resins found in the wreck were sticky organic substances that probably were to be used in perfume making.

It was difficult for archaeologists and historians to establish the ship's port of origin because so many different cultures were represented by its cargo. It is believed that the vessel was sailing from east to west. Kas, on the southwestern coast of Turkey, may have been the ship's intended port of call.

The excavation and study of the Uluburun Wreck were sponsored by the Institute of Nautical Archaeology (INA), a nonprofit scientific and educational organization based at Texas A & M University. Between 1984 and 1995, the INA conducted more than 22,000 dives to the Uluburun Wreck, most in water from 140 to 170 feet (43 to 52 meters) in depth. The INA is deeply concerned with artifact conservation and the scientific study of underwater remains.

Nautical archaeology is a relatively new science. The first underwater excavations involving archaeologically trained diving specialists took place in 1960. They were conducted by George Bass and other founding members of the INA.

"It's not merely discovery and recovery that concern us," says Corey Malcom, head archaeologist at the Mel Fisher Maritime Historical Society in Key West, Florida. "After all, we're trying to re-create the past as accurately as possible from what we find—to reconstruct a culture, perhaps.

"This means that standardized recovery and recording techniques have to be followed. This includes making diarylike accounts of the work being performed, photographing the various stages of recovery, and setting down detailed descriptions of the artifacts and the circumstances surrounding the recovery of each.

Archaeologists aboard the Institute of Nautical Archaeology (INA) research vessel Virazon *sift through the contents of an ancient amphora.*

"And these are only the first steps. There's the work that must follow in the conservation and preservation labs.

"Much of the material that's recovered from the underwater sites requires special treatment," Malcom points out. "There's an enormous amount of work to be done. For every day I'm at an underwater site, I spend two to three weeks in the lab doing conservation and research.

"Every site we approach is different," Malcom says. "You have to proceed with caution.

"High-tech submersibles and advanced electronic gear are great. But there's really no substitute for the human eye and hand in recovering and interpreting what's been discovered."

Nautical archaeologists were once limited to coastal waters and depths to 200 feet (60 meters) or so, as deep as scuba gear permitted them to go. But now manned submersibles, remotely controlled robots, and even a once-secret nuclear submarine are being used to take archaeologists deeper than ever before. Indeed, they have opened up a new era in maritime history.

Dr. Robert Ballard, known for his discovery of the *Titanic* in 1985, has helped to point the way. In 1988 and 1989, Dr. Ballard, using *Jason* and other underwater deep-diving robots, led expeditions to the Mediterranean Sea.

Dr. Ballard's most important discovery was made some 60 miles (97 kilometers) north of the North African city of Tunis, about half a mile down. There Dr. Ballard found a complete Roman ship of the fourth century.

The location of the wreck, not far from Sicily, indicated that the ship, undoubtedly a trading vessel, was sailing between Rome and Carthage, an ancient and powerful city-state in North Africa.

Jason *played an important part of Dr. Robert Ballard's discovery of a complete ancient Roman ship in the Mediterranean Sea.*

Using *Jason's* manipulator arm, Dr. Ballard recovered a treasure trove of artifacts from the vessel. They included ten amphoras, iron anchors, a grindstone, a cooking pot, a lamp made of clay decorated with a drawing of a running animal, and a copper coin from the reign of Roman emperor Constantine II (A.D. 355–361). Dr. Ballard and his team named the ship *Isis* after an ancient Egyptian goddess.[3]

The team also discovered evidence of other wrecked ships and countless artifacts strewn about the seafloor. The scientists recovered seventeen amphoras from the debris. The earliest was from the fourth century B.C.

Archaeologists who later examined the artifacts said that these objects indicated the existence of a busy trade route over the open sea between Rome and Carthage. It was previously thought that mariners of this early period seldom ventured out of sight of land because they feared storms.

Excited by what he had found and what had been learned, Dr. Ballard made plans to return to the site. When he did, he had at his disposal the NR (Nuclear Research)-1, a once-secret, deep-diving nuclear submarine.

The 146-foot (45-meter)-long vessel, powered by a nuclear reactor, was big enough to shelter and feed a crew of eleven and two scientists. It boasted lights, cameras, sensors, viewing portholes fitted into the ship's deck behind the control center, wheels that enabled the vessel to glide across the ocean bottom, and a powerful manipulator arm for retrieving objects from the seabed.

The NR-1, being nuclear powered, could stay down days, even weeks, at a time. The amount of time it could spend on the bottom was limited only by the amount of food being carried for those aboard.

The NR-1 had been launched by the United States in 1969. During the 1970s and 1980s it performed a variety of secret Cold War missions for the Navy. In 1976 it helped to salvage a Navy F-14 fighter plane and its Phoenix air-to-air missile, a mission that was cloaked in secrecy at the time. Once the Cold War ended, the Navy began making the NR-1 available for exploration and scientific research.

The NR-1, said Dr. John R. Humphrey, editor of *The Journal of Roman Archaeology*, would enable Dr. Ballard to "get to deeper spots than anybody else."

"Previous knowledge of trading routes was based on shallow-water work," said Dr. Humphrey. "This is going to change the whole map."[4]

Dr. Ballard returned to the Mediterranean aboard the NR-1 during the summer of 1997. Off the northwest coast of Sicily at a depth of more than half a mile, he and his team discovered the largest concentration of ancient shipwrecks ever found in the deep sea.[5]

One of the Roman ships carried a unique cargo. It consisted of huge marble columns and carefully cut blocks of stone. Some of the stones were notched so they could be fitted together. Archaeologists reasoned that the pieces may have represented a prefabricated temple.

While the wooden decks and upper hulls of several of the ships had been destroyed by wood-eating mollusks, timbers buried in the mud were in good condition, as was an array of artifacts. *Jason's* pilot maneuvered the robot arm as it picked up glassware, bronze vessels, and several different types of amphoras.

The wrecks were spread over an area of 20 square miles (52 square kilometers). In the area were the remains of five Roman ships and three sailing ships from relatively recent times. One was an Islamic ship from the late eighteenth to early nineteenth century. The other two were shipwrecks from the nineteenth century. Dr. Ballard called the area "a graveyard of ships spanning 2,000 years."[6]

Not only were there a great number of ships in the area, but the pieces to be recovered, since they were in deep water, promised to be in fairly good condition. In shallow water, artifacts can get pounded against rocks or reefs by waves. They also can get encrusted by coral or looted by treasure hunters. Dr. Ballard said he planned to do further exploration in the Mediterranean. He also announced plans to investigate shipping routes in the Black Sea.

Other scientists and treasure-seekers have their eyes on the Azores, a group of islands in the North Atlantic about 1,200 miles (1,930 kilometers) west of Portugal. The Azores frequently were the first stop for ships returning to Europe from the Americas. Often these vessels were heavily laden with New World riches—gold, silver, fine jewelry, porcelain, and china.

Hundreds of these ships, attacked by pirates or raked by storms, sank in the waters off the Azores. Dr. Francisco J. S. Alves, director of the National Museum of Archaeology in Lisbon, Portugal, calls the Azores "a kind of world sanctuary of underwater culture."[7]

Like the ancient Roman wrecks discovered by Dr. Ballard, these lost ships were long considered to be unreachable because they lay in very deep water. But since new submersibles and robots make deepwater recoveries possible, a dozen companies or groups are seeking to probe the waters of the Azores.

Archaeologists and historians are thus gaining knowledge of a multitude of ancient shipwrecks for the first time. A new world of discovery has opened.

7

TREASURE WRECK

They call it America's *Titanic*. To more than a few historians, the sinking of the luxury passenger steamer *Central America* in a ferocious hurricane off the coast of South Carolina in September 1857 was every bit as sensational in its own time as the loss of the great British liner in the North Atlantic almost fifty-five years later.

In some ways it was even more sensational. Bound from Panama to New York City, the *Central America* went down with 578 passengers and crew members; 425 people were lost. Many of the passengers had left San Francisco almost a month before after seeking their fortunes during the gold rush. Hundreds of millions of dollars in gold coins and bars slipped into the sea with them.

Losing all that gold sent shock waves through America's financial community. New York bankers had been waiting for a good portion of the gold to settle debts and back up loans. Its loss helped to trigger the Panic of 1857, one of America's most serious economic depressions.

Until recently, the riches of the *Central America* lay more than 1.5 miles (2.4 kilometers) below the surface. The deep location of the wreck discouraged anyone from looking for the vessel.

Then in 1985, a team of Columbus, Ohio, engineers and scientists, aware of the many advances in deep-diving technology, began mapping plans to locate the *Central America* and recover its awesome cargo.

The founder of the project was Thomas G. ("Tommy") Thompson, an engineer with previous experience in deep-water projects. His sister once recalled Tommy as the kind of kid who "was always dragging home neighbors' junk from the alley—old TVs, radios, motors—and coming up with new inventions."[1] Thompson was to put this talent to good use in the search for the *Central America*.

Thompson called upon two longtime friends, Barry Schatz, a writer at *The Miami Herald*, and Bob Evans, a geologist, to become members of his team. They called themselves the Columbus-America Discovery Group.

From the beginning, the three men were concerned with much more than gold. They realized that they would be investigating a shipwreck that had enormous historical and scientific value. They resolved that they would treat it as an archaeological site, retrieving all objects with the utmost care. Eventually more than fifty scientists from different parts of the world would be involved in studies concerning the wreck.[2]

As their first step, Thompson and his partners launched a determined search for every scrap of information regarding the *Central America* and the disaster that had befallen the vessel.

The *Central America* was a steamship that carried passengers and freight between New York and Panama. In those days, before the completion of a transcontinental railroad, such steamers offered the quickest and easiest method of travel between the east and west coasts of the United States.

Every two weeks, steamships left New York and San Francisco for the Isthmus of Panama, the narrow strip of land that separates the Pacific and Atlantic oceans. The ports on the opposite coasts of the Isthmus were linked by a railroad.

Upon arrival in Panama, passengers from San Francisco would board railroad cars for the three- to four-hour trip across the Isthmus where their New York-bound steamer was waiting. (The Panama Canal, which would eliminate the need for the railroad connection, would not begin operation for another fifty-seven years.) The same railroad transported newly arrived passengers from New York to the Pacific side.

Each year for some twenty years, beginning with the discovery of gold in California until the completion of the transcontinental railroad in 1869, thousands of passengers and tons of freight traveled what was called the Panama Route from New York and San Francisco. Gold, too, was shipped in huge quantities, some 2.9 million pounds (1.3 million kilograms) of it, during those two decades.[3]

The *Central America* was one of two steamships that served the Atlantic leg of the journey. The vessel was notable for its trim hull, almost as long as a football field, made of pine and oak covered with a thin layer of copper.

While it carried massive sails from its three towering masts, the *Central America* was also powered by a pair of huge steam engines that turned enormous paddle wheels, one on each side of the ship. Its cruising speed of 11 nautical miles (20 kilometers) an hour enabled the ship to make the round-trip voyage between New York and Panama in about twenty days.

During four years of operation, the *Central America* carried close to one-third of all the gold shipped from San Francisco to New York by way of Panama. In that time, the vessel made forty-three round-trip voyages between the two ports.

The forty-fourth began in normal fashion. The vessel steamed out of New York, then headed south, fringing the east coast of the United States. After rounding the southern tip of Florida and then the western tip of Cuba, the *Central America* sailed directly south to Panama.

On September 3, 1857, the 477 passengers, who had left San Francisco two weeks before, were brought to the dock where they boarded the *Central America*, which left Panama that afternoon.

The ship arrived in Havana, Cuba, four days later to take on coal, and departed the following morning. "We left Havana at 9 o'clock in the morning of the 8th instant, with clear weather and every prospect of a pleasant passage," J. A. Foster, a passenger, noted.[4]

The clear weather did not last long. Virginia Birch, another passenger, reported, "On the day after we left Havana, I, with other ladies, were on deck, but a squall came up, and the wind blew like a whirlwind, and we had to go downstairs."[5]

"Toward night, the seamen began to call it a storm," another of the ship's passengers remembered.

For three days, the ship pitched and rocked in mountainous seas. "Down below . . . nothing was to be heard but the crying of children and the moans of those suffering seasickness," said a passenger, "and rising above all the sounds . . . was the continued dashing and splashing of the waves against the sides of the ship, and the howling of the storm as the wind surged through the steamer's rigging."[6]

As the violence of the storm increased, the winds tore the sails to shreds, and the ship began to leak. Male passengers helped the crew in bailing with buckets.

On the morning of September 12 the clouds lifted, and some crew members felt the worst was over. But not Captain William Lewis Herndon. He told one of the passengers that there was no hope unless the storm died down or some other vessel appeared upon the scene.

About noon that day, a small sailing vessel, the *Marine*, was spotted. Captain Herndon ordered all women and children into the *Central America*'s lifeboats. Miraculously, the small boats made their way through the churning water to the *Marine*. All of the women passengers and all but one of the children were saved.

That evening, the *Central America* began to sink. "All at once," one of the women aboard the *Marine* was to recall, "the ship made a plunge at an angle of forty-five degrees, and then disappeared forever. . . ." Some 425 passengers and crew members drowned in what was the worst peacetime loss of life ever suffered by an American ship at sea.

Eight hours after the *Central America* sank, the Norwegian sailing ship *Ellen* plowed into the area to find dozens of survivors in their life preservers, many clinging to floating wreckage. The *Ellen* took fifty of the *Central America*'s passengers aboard.

When Tommy Thompson and the other members of his Columbus-America team began to reconstruct what had happened to the *Central America,* several sources of information were immediately available. They had accounts of the disaster from newspapers of the day, including interviews with many of the survivors. They had copies of letters written by those who had survived. They also were able to get reports that had been issued by government agencies that had investigated the tragedy.

By consulting newspaper accounts of the disaster that quoted the captains of vessels that were close to the *Central America* when the ship went down, Thompson and his team were able to get navigational data about the ship. This helped the team in pinpointing the approximate location of the wreck.

Information about the storm that raged that day was also critical. How did the fierce winds and ocean currents affect the position of the vessel? The Columbus-America team also obtained information about the *Central America* from lighthouses in the area.

All of the information was fed into computers. "Probability maps" generated by the computers indicated that the wreck was likely to be found about 200 miles (320 kilometers) off the coast of South Carolina within an area of 1,400 square miles (3,626 square kilometers) known as Blake Ridge.

With the target area established, the search entered a new phase that involved surveying a chunk of the ocean floor almost the size of the state of Rhode Island. The area was divided into "cells," each a half-mile square. Most of the cells were assigned a number between 1 and 10,000. The higher the number a cell was given, the greater the likelihood it would contain the remains of the *Central America.*

The search began in earnest during the summer of 1986. Thompson, Schatz, and Evans chartered a boat and with the help of electronic experts outfitted the vessel with an advanced sonar system. The state-of-the-art sonar equipment had been developed during the mid-1970s for use in the search for undersea mineral deposits.

The equipment included a pontoon-shaped device that was to be towed at the end of a cable 1,500 feet (457 meters) above the seafloor. The sonar signal it emit-

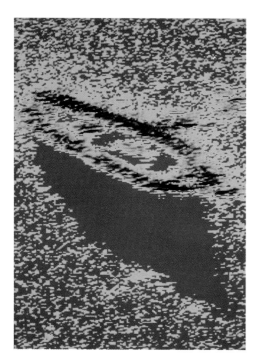

Side-scan sonar produced this image of the Central America *as it rested on the ocean bottom.*

ted covered a 3-mile (5-kilometer) strip of ocean bottom on each pass. The Columbus team hoped that its sonar would respond to the boiler, engines, or other large clumps of iron that were part of the *Central America*, just as Dr. Robert Ballard had used *Argo's* sonar system in seeking out the location of the *Titanic*.

For forty days Thompson and his team crisscrossed the target area. The search produced several sonar images that looked very promising, including one that might be a side-wheel steamship.

After the search ended, the team returned to Columbus, Ohio, to begin construction of a massive undersea robot vehicle. It was to play a leading role in the recovery of the *Central America's* mountain of gold and historical riches.

Named *Nemo* after the legendary captain of Jules Verne's novel *Twenty Thousand Leagues Under the Sea*, it was different from *Alvin* and *Argo* equipment in that all the researchers stayed on the surface. *Nemo*, in fact, was the first remotely operated exploratory vehicle capable of performing heavy work in the deep ocean.

The 12,000-pound (5,443-kilogram) *Nemo*, about the size of a pickup truck, bristled with an assortment of wires and tubes, lights and thrusters, and powerful robotic arms and hands. Unlike the Russian submersibles *Mir I* and *Mir II*, which are noted for their sleekness, *Nemo* looked like a clunky piece of abstract sculpture that had been created by an artist who combed junkyards for his parts.

But the robot's ungainly appearance was misleading. It was capable of performing an array of underwater tasks, some of them delicate.

With its robotic arm, precision manipulators, and suction-cup fingers, *Nemo* was designed to recover items as large as a 1,000-pound (454-kilogram) anchor or as small as a gold coin the size of a dime. For retrieving loosely grouped items, such as stacked coins, from the ocean floor, *Nemo* would rely on a clever "slime machine." It would cover the pieces in a fast-hardening silicone solution within a mold, then bring them to the surface as a single lump.

This mass of gold coins and bars—plus the tiny starfish—were found amid the wreckage of the Central America.

Nemo was to be linked to the mother ship at the surface by 10,000 feet (3,048 meters) of coaxial cable. Through the cable would flow data from the robot's television cameras and sensors to engineers seated before television monitors in the mother ship's control room, who would be directing the dive.

Before *Nemo* was sent to the bottom from the mother ship, a network of sonar transmitters was to be planted on the ocean floor encircling the wreck site. Through the use of these signaling devices, called transponders, engineers would be able to carefully position *Nemo* for each chore that it would be called upon to perform.

During the summer of 1987, *Nemo* was taken to sea to probe the highest probability cells. The Columbus team had acquired a research vessel, the *Arctic Discoverer*, from which *Nemo* was to be launched and recovered. Its control room boasted seventeen video screens that were to be used in monitoring the seafloor and the submersible.

In August, as *Nemo's* pilot aboard the *Arctic Discoverer* maneuvered the submersible over the flat seabed, the image of a steamship's side wheel suddenly appeared on one of the TV screens. The engineers and scientists shrieked with joy. "It

On its dive to the wreck site, *Nemo's* cameras captured many fascinating glimpses of deep-sea marine life. One day a 21-foot (6-meter)-long Greenland shark drifted by the camera lens. The sighting was bizarre because the creature was almost 1,000 miles (1,600 kilometers) farther south than a shark of that species had ever been seen before.[9]

In a scientific experiment to attract undersea predators, *Nemo* deposited several food trays heaped with fish carcasses on the seabed. Before long, scores of monkey-faced eels were seen feeding on the carcasses. When *Nemo* later returned to the scene, a few of the fish carcasses remained, but the trays that the scientists had put down were gone. It was thought that the trays had been devoured by the Greenland shark, a creature known to eat almost anything.

Many of the exotic and colorful sea creatures viewed by *Nemo's* cameras had never been observed before. And a number of new species of undersea life were found at the wreck site, including five new species of sponge.

was a special moment," said Bob Evans, "as if the wreck were calling to us: 'Here I am.'"[7]

In the days that followed, the team recovered a number of artifacts from the site, including the ship's bell. These confirmed that the ship was indeed the *Central America*.

When the team returned to the site in 1989, serious recovery work began. *Nemo* made dozens of dives, picking up hundreds of gold bars and thousands of gold coins. The submersible also brought back gold dust, flakes, and nuggets, and on one dive returned with a gold bar that weighed more than 62 pounds (28 kilograms). "It's like a storybook treasure in a kid's book," said Tommy Thompson. "I never dreamed it would be like this."[8]

Hundreds of gold coins were hauled up from the wreckage. Many of these were twenty-dollar gold pieces, a coin slightly larger than today's half-dollar. Such coins are known as double eagles. Each is valued at many hundreds of dollars.

The coin finds included a neat stack of three hundred double eagles. Originally the coins had filled a container, which had disintegrated over the years. But *Nemo* managed to recover the stack intact. Extremely rare fifty-dollar coins, minted in 1851, were also recovered.

Nemo recovered crystal goblets, corked bottles of beer, a porcelain washbasin, the base of a brass lamp that still contained some oil, and the lid from a jar of Roussel's Unrivaled Premium Shaving Cream.

The 37-degree Fahrenheit (3-degree Celsius) water at the sea bottom helped to preserve several large leather passenger trunks. Some contained the most valued possessions owned by families who were journeying to New York to establish new lives for themselves.

Besides clothes and personal items, one trunk held a pair of pistols, their barrels rusted away, a checkbook, a readable copy of *The New York News* for July 10, 1857, and a ceramic jar that contained Highly Perfumed Bear's Grease for Beautifying and Strengthening the Hair.[10] Bob Evans called the trunks "ultimate time capsules."

Late in September the waters of the Atlantic began to grow rough because of Hurricane Hugo. The Columbus-America group agreed to halt recovery operations and return home.

When the *Arctic Discoverer* arrived in Norfolk, Virginia, on October 5, 1989, several hundred people were waiting at dockside to greet the vessel. The huge crowd included family members of the crew as well as a throng of TV and newspaper reporters.

The arrival of the *Arctic Discoverer* also attracted lawyers representing thirty-nine insurance companies that claimed they had insured the gold in 1857. When the *Central America* sank, the companies said that they had covered the losses by reimbursing policyholders. The gold belonged to them, the insurance companies declared, and they wanted it.

Several years of law-court combat followed. A judge tossed out most of the insurance company claims for "lack of merit." It was eventually ruled that the Columbus-America group was entitled to 92.22 percent of the gold, the insurance companies to 7.78 percent.

As of 1998, no one knew exactly what the vast treasure was worth. Estimates of its value have run as high as $1 billion. Although no precise figure may be known for years, no one disputes the fact that it is "the greatest treasure ever found."

The *Titanic* was discovered in 1985 and the *Central America* in 1988. The *I-52*, a World War II Japanese submarine carrying more than two tons of gold, was found more than 3 miles (5 kilometers) below the surface of the Atlantic near the Cape Verde Islands in 1995. Efforts to find other richly historic vessels lost in the ocean's depths are sure to be made in the years ahead. Indeed, the *Titanic, Central America,* and *I-52* are merely the beginning.

Since the time of its sinking in 1912, the Titanic *has gripped the fascination of millions. This still photo from the 1997 movie "Titanic" shows the "unsinkable" ship going down.*

8

THE TITANIC: DISCOVERY AND REDISCOVERY

Ever since the dark, moonless night in April 1912, when the huge and "unsinkable" liner rammed an iceberg and plunged beneath the surface of the North Atlantic bringing death to 1,500 people, the *Titanic* has had a powerful grip on people's imagination.

More than one hundred books have been written about the ship. The *Titanic* has been the subject of at least two dozen movies. James Cameron's film "Titanic," released in 1997, became Hollywood's first billion-dollar movie and triggered a great wave of *Titanic*-mania that engulfed not only the United States but also much of the rest of the world.

In the years that followed its sinking, scientists and treasure hunters also felt the *Titanic*'s lure, and dreamed of finding the vessel. But turning those dreams into reality was no easy task, largely because its precise location was a mystery.

Although several serious attempts were made to find the liner, none succeeded. The discovery of the ship was kept waiting until the development of sophisticated navigation satellites and deep-diving submersibles that could probe the blackness of the ocean 2.5 miles (4 kilometers) down.

Jack Grimm, a wealthy Texas oilman, achieved some measure of fame for his efforts in attempting to pinpoint the vessel's location. Grimm, who died in 1998, spent millions of dollars in sponsoring several expeditions to the North Atlantic in the early 1980s.

After a search in 1981, Grimm claimed to have found the ship. He said his undersea photographs depicted the liner's anchor and one of its enormous propellers. But the pictures were grainy and unclear, and Grimm's claims were doubted.

At the same time that Jack Grimm was looking for the *Titanic*, Dr. Robert Ballard entered the scene. A scientist from Woods Hole Oceanographic Institution, Ballard once worked as a porpoise trainer at Sea Life Park in Hawaii and had been interested in the *Titanic* for well over a decade.

In the late 1970s, Ballard had proposed finding and photographing the vessel with an undersea camera that would be lowered on lengths of drill pipe from a research vessel at the surface. But when he tested the idea, the drill pipe broke. Ballard also considered descending to the *Titanic* in the submersible *Alvin*.

Ballard's plans for finding the *Titanic* got a big boost in 1982 when he received $2.8 million in funding from the U.S. Navy to develop and test an advanced underwater robot.[1] With the money, Ballard built *Argo*, the tethered robot about the size of an automobile that was designed to be controlled from a mother ship on the surface. He outfitted *Argo* with searchlights, video cameras, still cameras, and sonar.

To help him pinpoint the *Titanic*'s location, Ballard turned to French scientists who operated a state-of-the-art sonar system. During the summer of 1985, Ballard and the French spent twenty-two days combing about 80 percent of a 150-square-mile (389-square-kilometer) search area that they had laid out in the North Atlantic. But they found nothing.

After the French departed, Ballard kept trying. Later in the summer he again departed for the target area, this time aboard the *Knorr*, a Navy oceanographic ship. His team included twenty-two scientists, three of them from the original French group. Ballard's plan was to survey the remaining portion of the search area, the 20 percent not covered by the French team.

Besides having *Argo*, Ballard's team was aided by a military navigation satellite called Navstar. Navstar enabled the *Knorr's* navigators to maintain a precise knowledge of the vessel's position at all times during the search.

Aboard the *Knorr*, technicians in groups of seven stared at black-and-white television screens that were linked to *Argo* as the robot scanned the ocean bottom. For six days, they saw almost nothing but mud.

Ballard realized that almost a month had passed, and his team had not found the slightest clue to the *Titanic's* whereabouts. He was beginning to have his doubts. Perhaps, he thought, they had made mistakes in laying out the target area.

At 11:49 P.M. on August 31, Ballard's luck abruptly changed when a dark cloud appeared in the corner of one of the television monitors. "Here's something!" a technician declared.

The cloud got bigger. "It's coming in," he said.

Now everyone had their eyes glued to the monitor. Soon other cloudlike images began to appear, then odd shapes, then something huge and circular. "Look at it!" said a technician.

"God, it looks like. . ."

"The boiler!"

"It's a boiler!"[2]

The *Argo's* cameras were focusing on one of the *Titanic's* twenty-nine huge boilers. In these, water was heated to make steam for the ship's engines.

Everyone began to laugh and shout. Ballard had gone to bed. The *Knorr's* cook ran to get him.

Pulling on a blue jumpsuit over his pajamas, Ballard rushed to the scene. As soon as he glanced at the monitor, he knew that they had accomplished what many had said was impossible.

Ballard's research team took hundreds of feet of videotape and more than 12,000 color photographs of the wreckage. The pictures confirmed the claim of several

Dr. Robert Ballard, who discovered the location of the Titanic *in 1985, points out the features of* Jason Senior, *an undersea robot introduced in 1988.*

Titanic survivors that the ship had broken into several sections on the surface. The forward section and the stern now lay about half a mile apart, pointing in opposite directions.

Ballard's discovery of the *Titanic* in the summer of 1985 did not end the story. In fact, it signaled a new beginning. In the years since, countless expeditions have been organized to photograph the wreck or salvage its artifacts.

After their discovery of the *Titanic*, Ballard and the others aboard the *Knorr* tried to keep the site a secret from those seeking to cash in on the disaster. In all ship-to-shore communications from the *Knorr*, Ballard was careful not to give the exact location of the research vessel.

But it didn't take long for outsiders to outwit Ballard. One day, an unidentified private plane circled over the *Knorr* for more than an hour. According to a *Knorr* crew member, the aircraft was "nailing down the position" of the *Titanic*.

Ballard himself returned to the *Titanic* in the summer of 1986. This time he planned to dive down to the liner aboard *Alvin*. Linked to the submersible would be a new ROV, *Jason Junior*, which was equipped with powerful floodlights and a video camera capable of recording sixty hours of tape. Ballard called *Jason Junior* a "swimming eyeball."

The expedition was a huge success. *Alvin* made a total of twelve dives from its mother ship, spending thirty-two hours on the bottom.

Jason Junior photographed areas within the wreck that would have been hazardous for *Alvin* to enter. The stunning footage was used in the production of an hourlong videocassette called "Secrets of the *Titanic*."

Besides *Jason Junior* and its video camera, Ballard's team also controlled a camera sled, called *Angus*, that was tethered by an electronic cable to the mother ship. They steered *Angus* back and forth just above the *Titanic*'s bow and stern sections. On each pass, *Angus*'s three still cameras clicked away, taking more than 70,000 pictures. Later, more than a hundred of these images were assembled in such a way as to create a dramatic photo mosaic of the forward section of the wreck.[3]

Ballard, pilot Ralph Hollis, and technician Martin Bowen looked through *Alvin*'s portholes at the massive wreckage of the hull, which was draped with rusty icicles. Ballard called them "rusticles." The *Titanic*'s wooden deck was gone, consumed by generations of wood borers, such as worms, beetles, and mollusks.

Alvin crossed an area the size of a football field that was littered with debris from the *Titanic*. There were cups, saucers, plates, and bottles of wine, as well as large copper pots and pans from the ship's galleys.

"It's actually like going into a museum," said Ballard. "There are thousands and thousands of items all over the bottom."[4]

Some items had floated down after heavier pieces had already hit the seafloor. For example, Ballard spotted a teacup perched atop one of the ship's boilers. Obviously, the cup had drifted down after the boiler had landed on the bottom.

Ballard saw no bodies or bones. "The closest we saw was a shoe," he said, "no human remains, which was sort of a relief."[5]

The next year, 1987, a group of American investors joined forces with a French team to dive down to the *Titanic* in the French submersible *Nautile*. Their goal, however, was not to videotape or take still pictures of the wreck. They were after artifacts.

The French made thirty-two dives in *Nautile* that summer and brought some 1,800 objects to the surface. These included a porthole, a ship's bell, a safe, a compass, and a leather bag that was found to contain jewelry.

RMS Titanic Inc., of New York City, the company that sponsored the salvage expedition in 1987, was granted ownership of the *Titanic* by being the first to recover artifacts. The company and their French team returned to the wreck site in 1993, 1994, and 1996.[6]

The 1996 expedition made headlines. Working from *Nautile* and its mother ship, *Nadir*, the salvage team attempted to raise a section of the *Titanic*'s hull, a chunk of steel almost as big as half a tennis court and weighing 11 tons. The steel section included four complete portholes and the remains of four others.

At the surface, four enormous lift bags were filled with diesel fuel, which is lighter than water. The bags were then attached to bundles of steel chains weighing 25 tons. The chains dragged the lift bags to the bottom.

There, technicians aboard *Nautile* took over. Using the submersible's powerful manipulator arms, they attached cables from the four lift bags to the steel plate. According to the plan, when the bundles of chains were released from the lift bags, the bags would rise to the surface, thereby lifting the hull plate.[7]

Once at the surface, the hull section was to be loaded onto a barge. The barge would be towed to shore, and, later, brought to New York Harbor. By doing this, the salvors intended to bring a symbolic end to the voyage of the *Titanic*, which had begun in Southampton, England, eighty-four years before. The hull plate was eventually to become the feature attraction in a *Titanic* museum.

The salvage team's plans went awry, however. They managed to get the hull plate to within less than 100 feet (30 meters) of the surface, but bad weather developed and the seas became rough. They then decided to try to tow the section closer to shore, where the water would be calmer. But the stormy seas tore two of the lift bags away from the hull plate, and it sank back to the ocean floor.

"Getting the hull up as far as we did was amazing," said George Tulloch, who headed the salvage effort for RMS Titanic. "The fact that it slipped is really a small failure in our mind. We'll try again."[8]

Tulloch's team had the foresight to attach an acoustic device to the hull plate. During the summer of 1998, its beeping guided Tulloch and his team to where the hull plate had landed. They were successful in raising the piece, which was brought to Boston where it was put on exhibition.

Many of those who made the 2.5-mile (4-kilometer) journey to the *Titanic's* resting place during the 1990s did so in submersibles and deep-diving robots that were outfitted with advanced cameras and powerful lights. They had little interest in conducting scientific investigation and less in recovering souvenirs. They were there to photograph the wreckage and the debris from the vessel that is strewn about the ocean floor.

A Canadian-American-Russian photographic team descended to the *Titanic* in 1991. This venture produced spectacular results. Working from the pair of Russian submersibles, *Mir I* and *Mir II*, and using state-of-the-art mercury-vapor lamps, the team lit up a large expanse of the wreck site for the first time.

The sweeping views that they were able to film were only part of it. They also made stereo images of the liner that led to the production of a three-dimensional motion picture.

Called "Titanica," it was released in 1993. A Canadian newspaper, *The Ottawa Citizen*, described it as being "eerie and awesome."

James Cameron, producer and director of the movie "Titanic," dived down to the *Titanic* in 1995, also using *Mir I* and *Mir II*, to photograph the wreck. He then used some of the footage in his movie.

From a production standpoint, "Titanic" was an extremely complex film, which used amazing visual effects that were generated by computers. There are, in fact, 400 to 500 digital shots in the film.

This striking photograph of the Titanic's bow was taken in 1991 during the filming of "Titanica."

Cameron was once asked if there was one shot in the movie that he is more proud of than any other, one that called for the utmost in terms of technical and artistic ability. "I can't choose one shot over another," Cameron said, "but what pushed me to the limit was the Grand Staircase of the *Titanic*.[9]

Cameron was referring to a scene in which his robot camera picked its way through the narrow passages of the ship's interior to photograph what remained of the *Titanic*'s magnificent stairwell, which descended from the ship's upper decks to its reception area and grand salon. The cameras focused on hand-carved oak columns and finely detailed wood paneling in a remarkable state of preservation. "That's something that nobody ever did before," said Cameron, "so I take more pride in that than all the digital stuff."

Cameron spent two years putting together what he called the first-ever Hollywood deep-diving expedition. It consisted of many different elements. One of the most important was the research vessel *Akademik Mstislav Keldysh*, the largest ship of its kind in the world. The *Keldysh* served as mother ship for *Mir I* and *Mir II*. One of these submersibles filmed the wreckage, while the other operated the underwater lighting system.

The expedition's equipment also included a tethered robot. Called *Snoop Dog*, it carried housing to protect a specially built motion-picture camera from deepwater pressure. The camera was equipped with a "pan-tilt" device that enabled it to move in a natural manner when filming.

The production crew, according to Cameron, comprised Russian, Canadian, and American engineers, film technicians, marine scientists, and hard-core seafarers. "Each dive was planned like a lunar mission," said Cameron, "with hours spent simulating the movement of the [submersibles] with miniatures and video systems, with charts and diagrams and shot lists issued to each [submersible] team before each dive."[10]

Cameron and his cameraman made a dozen dives to the *Titanic*. Each required a two-and-a-half hour descent, which was followed by ten to twelve hours of concentrated effort as he and his technicians positioned the two submersibles, the cameras, and lights. On the last day of production, *Snoop Dog* was used to film the grand staircase.

In the years ahead, with improvements in lights and cameras, the *Titanic* is certain to give up even more of its secrets to filmmakers.

But it is not only film producers who are enticed to visit the great liner. Those two halves of rusting steel, a half a mile apart, will continue to lure an army of scientists, engineers, archaeologists, historians, treasure hunters, and the merely curious into the black depths of the North Atlantic.

Sunken vessels such as the *Titanic* represent only a small part of the challenge. "We know more about distant galaxies than we do about two-thirds of our own planet," said Bruce Robison, a noted oceanographer at the Monterey Bay Aquarium Research Institute, referring to the oceans. "It'll be decades before we truly begin to understand [the oceans], the most complex environment on earth."[11]

Much progress is being made. The submersibles, remote-controlled vehicles, and newly developed autonomous seafloor observatories have already helped to give us a more advanced understanding of the physical and chemical makeup of the world's oceans and the animals and plants that inhabit them. The way has been paved for continued exploration that is certain to lead to even more exciting and significant discoveries.

SOURCE NOTES

CHAPTER 1, EXPLORING THE DEEP SEA

1. Walter Sullivan, "Divers Report No Hull Gash in the *Titanic*," *The New York Times*, July 31, 1986, p. 1.

2. Joseph Wallace, *The Deep Sea*. New York: Gallery Books, 1987, p. 87.

3. William J. Broad, *The Universe Below: Discovering the Secrets of the Deep Sea*. New York: Simon and Schuster, 1997, p. 49.

4. Ibid., p. 55.

CHAPTER 2, *ALVIN, ARGO*, AND BEYOND

1. "The Last Frontier," *Time*, August 14, 1995, p. 54.

2. William J. Broad, *The Universe Below, Discovering the Secrets of the Deep Sea*. New York: Simon and Schuster, 1997, p. 147.

3. Ibid., p. 272.

4. Joseph Wallace, *The Deep Sea*. New York: Gallery Books, 1987, p. 56.

5. Abe Dane, "Robots of the Deep," *Popular Mechanics*, June 1993, p. 104.

6. Ibid., p. 105.

CHAPTER 3, WEIRD LIFE IN THE DEEP SEA

1. Malcolm W. Browne, "Fish That Dates Back to the Age of Dinosaurs Is Facing Extinction," *The New York Times*, April 18, 1995, p. C4.

2. Ibid.

3. Ibid.

4. Phil Long, "Cuban Fish Tale Makes History," *The Miami Herald*, January 12, 1998, p. 8A.

5. Ibid.

6. William J. Broad, "Biologists Closing in on Lair of Giant Squid," *The New York Times*, February 13, 1996, p. C1.

7. William J. Broad, "Squids Emerge as Smart, Elusive Hunters of the Mid-Sea," *The New York Times*, August 30, 1994, p. C6.

8. Broad, op. cit., February 13, 1996, p. C9.

9. Broad, op. cit., August 30, 1994, p. C6.

CHAPTER 4, HOT WATER IN THE COLD SEA

1. Victoria A. Kaharl, *Water Baby: The Story of* Alvin. New York: Oxford University Press, 1990, p. 319.

2. Ibid.

3. William J. Broad, *The Universe Below: Discovering the Secrets of the Deep Sea*. New York: Simon and Schuster, 1997, p. 262.

4. William J. Broad, "Undersea Treasure and Its Odd Guardians," *The New York Times*, December 20, 1997, p. F1.

5. William J. Broad, "First Move Made to Mine Mineral Riches of Seabed," *The New York Times*, December 21, 1997, p. 1.

CHAPTER 5, BIRTH OF AN ISLAND

1. Noreen Parks, "Loihi Rumbles to Life," *Earth*, April 1997, p. 43.

2. Ibid., p. 44.

3. Kathy Sawyer, "Next Hawaiian Island Taking Shape," *The Washington Post*, October 5, 1996, p. A14.

4. Jan TenBruggencatem "Loihi's Secret: A Little Known Form of Life," *The Honolulu Advertiser*, October 13, 1996, p. 1.

CHAPTER 6, DIVING INTO HISTORY

1. George F. Bass, "Oldest Known Shipwreck Reveals Splendors of the Bronze Age," *National Geographic*, December 1987, p. 700.

2. Ibid., p. 695.

3. John Noble Wilford, "Roman Ships Found Off Sicily; New Sites Broaden Study," *The New York Times*, July 31, 1997, p. A3.

4. William J. Broad, "Secret Sub to Scan Sea Floor for Roman Wrecks," *The New York Times*, February 7, 1995, p. C1.

5. Wilford, op. cit., *The New York Times*, July 31, 1997.

6. Ibid.

7. William J. Broad, "Watery Grave of the Azores to Yield Shipwreck Riches," *The New York Times*, June 6, 1995, p. Cl.

CHAPTER 7, TREASURE WRECK

1. Tim Noonan, "The Greatest Treasure Ever Found," *Life*, March 1992, p. 35.

2. Ibid., p. 40.

3. Judy Conrad, Editor, *Story of an American Tragedy*. Columbus, Ohio: Columbus-America Discovery Group, 1988, p. xiii.

4. Ibid., p. 17.

5. Ibid., p. 18.

6. Ibid.

7. Noonan, op. cit., p. 37.

8. Ken Ringle, "'Storybook Treasure' Found Off South Carolina," *The Washington Post*, September 14, 1989, p. 1.

9. Charles H. Herdendorf, "Discovering an Alien Environment," *American History Illustrated*, March/April 1991, p. 71.

10. Ibid.

CHAPTER 8, THE *TITANIC*: DISCOVERY AND REDISCOVERY

1. Victoria A. Kaharl, *Water Baby: The Story of Alvin*. New York: Oxford University Press, 1990, p. 284.

2. Ibid., p. 285.

3. Robert D. Ballard, "Epilogue for *Titanic*," *National Geographic*, October 1987, p. 454.

4. Kaharl, op. cit., p. 294.

5. Ibid.

6. William J. Broad, "Titanic Relics Open Era in Deep-Sea Commerce," *The New York Times*, August 25, 1996, p. 24.

7. Randy Kennedy, "With Ship's Hull Back on Ocean Floor, *Titanic* Buffs Return to New York," *The New York Times*, September 2, 1996, p. 26.

8. Ibid.

9. Alex Gove, "Titanic Ambition," *The Red Herring*, January 1998, p. 78.

10. *James Cameron's* Titanic. New York: HarperCollins, 1997, p. ix.

11. Joseph Wallace, *The Deep Sea*, New York: Gallery Books, 1987, p. 9.

FOR MORE INFORMATION

Private Research Organizations

Harbor Branch Oceanographic
Institution
5600 U.S. 1 North
Fort Pierce, Florida 34946
(561) 465-2400
www.hboi.edu
Based at a 500-acre (200-hectare) facility in southeastern
Florida, Harbor Branch pursues
underwater research and
development through seven
different operating divisions:
Aquaculture, Marine Operations, Biomedical Marine
Research, Engineering, Marine
Science, Marine Education,
and Environmental Laboratory.

Institute of Nautical Archaeology
P.O. Drawer HG
College Station, Texas 77841
(409) 845-6694
www.nautcal@tamu.edu
A nonprofit scientific and
educational organization affiliated with Texas A & M University, the Institute has sponsored
more than twenty undersea
archaeological projects in more
than a dozen nations since its
founding in 1973.

Monterey Bay Aquarium
Research Institute (MBARI)
770 Sandholdt Road
Moss Landing, California 95039
(831) 775-1700
www.mbari.org
On the California coast south of
San Francisco, MBARI focuses
on oceanographic research in
areas beyond relatively shallow
coastal waters.

National Center for Shipwreck
Research
P.O. Box 2574
Key Largo, Florida 33037
(305) 453-3833
members.aol.com/rreddog999
A nonprofit research and
education organization, the
National Center has been
involved in shipwreck exploration and research in the Florida
Straits, Gulf of Mexico, and
Caribbean since 1985.

Scripps Oceanographic
Institution
University of California,
San Diego
A-033B
La Jolla, California 92093
(619) 534-1294
A branch of the University of
California, Scripps is one of the
world's foremost centers for
ocean research, particularly in
deep-sea areas.

Woods Hole Oceanographic
Institution
Woods Hole, Massachusetts
02543
(508) 548-1400
www.whoi.edu
Located on Cape Cod, Woods
Hole investigates all aspects of
oceanography and, chiefly
through its operation of *Alvin*,
Jason, and other vehicles and
vessels, has been at the fore-
front in undersea exploration,
discovery, and research.

FEDERAL AGENCIES

National Oceanic and Atmo-
spheric Administration (NOAA)
Commerce Department
14th Street and Constitution
Avenue, N.W.
Washington, DC 20230
(202) 482-4901
A branch of the Commerce
Department, NOAA, through its
Ocean and Coastal Resource
Management division and its
division of Ocean Resources,
Conservation, and Assessment,
conducts a wide range of
research projects in deep-
ocean waters.

National Science Foundation
(NSF)
4201 Wilson Boulevard
Arlington, Virginia 22230
(703) 306-1234
www.nsf.gov
A federal agency that provides
funding for basic scientific
research and has served as a
principal sponsor of *Alvin*
expeditions.

U. S. Geological Survey
Department of the Interior
1849 C Street, N.W.
Washington, DC 20240
(202) 208-3171
A branch of the Department of
the Interior, the USGS conducts
research on mineral deposits
and the structure of the earth
both on land and at sea.

MARINE MUSEUMS

Inland Seas Maritime Museum
Great Lakes Historical Society
480 Main Street
P.O. Box 435
Vermilion, Ohio 44089
(440) 967-3467
www.inlandseas.org

The Mariners' Museum
100 Museum Drive
Newport News, Virginia 23606
(757) 596-2222
www.mariner.org

Maritime Aquarium at Norwalk
10 North Water Street
Norwalk, Connecticut 06854
(203) 852-0700
www.maritimeaquarium.org

Mel Fisher Maritime Heritage
Society
200 Greene Street
Key West, Florida 33040
(305) 294-4035

Mystic Seaport Museum
75 Greenmanville Avenue
Mystic, Connecticut 06355
(860) 572-0711
www.myticseaport.org

New York Aquarium
Surf Avenue & West 8th Street
Brooklyn, New York 11224
(718) 265-3474
www.nyaquarium.com

South Street Seaport Museum
207 Front Street
New York, NY 10038
(212) 748-8600
www.southstseaport.org

INDEX

Page numbers in *italics* refer to illustrations.

ABE (Autonomous Benthic
    Explorer), 21, *22*, 23
Akademik Mstislav Keldysh
    (research vessel), 71
Alves, Francisco J.S., 52
Alvin (submersible), 7, *8*, 9, 14-
    19, *17*, 34, 35, 38, 58, 64, 67
American Museum of Natural
    History, 30
amphoras, 45, 50
Angus (camera sled), 67
Arctic Discoverer (research
    vessel), 59, 61
Argo (sonar sled), 19-20, 58, 64,
    65
Atlantis (research vessel), 16, 18
Atocha (Spanish galleon), 21
AUVs (autonomous under-
    water vehicles), 21, 23

Azores, 51-52

Ballard, Robert, 7, 8, 19, 45, 48,
    50-52, 58, 64-67, *66*
ballast tanks, 16
Barton, Otis, 11
Bass, George, 47
bathyscaph, 12-13
bathysphere, *11*, 11-12
Beebe, William, 11-12
Binns, Ray, 38
Birch, Virginia, 56
Black Sea, 51
black smokers, 35, 38
Bowen, Martin, 67

Cameron, James, 63, 69, 71
Cape Verde Islands, 61
Central America (steamship),
    53-61, *58*
cephalopods, 29
Challenger Deep, 14

Challenger (space shuttle), 27
chemosynthesis, 34
Christmas tree worms, *32*
clams, 33, 34
coelacanths, 24-26, *25*, 25, 31
Cold War, 36, 50
Columbus-America Discovery
    Group, 54, 57-61
Cousteau, Jacques, 10, 11
crabs, 33, 34
Cuba, 27

diving, technology of, 10-12
Duennebier, Fred, 39-41

Earle, Sylvia A., 15, 38
East Pacific Rise, 20
Ellen (sailing vessel), 56
Evans, Bob, 54, 57, 60, 61

Fisher, Mel, 20-21
Forch, Ellen C., 31

fossils, 24
Foster, J.A., 56
Fricke, Hans, 24-26
fringe finned fish, 26

Gagnon, Émile, 10
Galápagos Islands, 33-35
giant squid, 29-32, *30*
Gilmore, Grant, 27
goby fish, 27, 31
Godzilla, 35
Gorda Ridge, 35-36
Grand Comore Island, 25, 26
Greeks, ancient, 10
Greenland shark, 60
Grimm, Jack, 64
gulper eel, 25

H.M.S. *Challenger* (sailing ship), 9-10, 14
Herndon, William Lewis, 56
Hessler, Bob, 34
Hollis, Ralph, 34, 67
Humphrey, John R., 50-51
hydrothermal vents, 23, 33-36, 38, 41, 42

I-52 (Japanese submarine), 61
information sources, 76-77
ingots, 45
Institute of Nautical Archaeology (INA), 47, 48
Isis (Roman ship), 48, 50

Jason (robot), 20, 48, *49*, 50
Jason Junior (robot), 7, 20, 67
Jason Senior (robot), *66*
Johnson Sea Link (submersible), 27, *28*, 31

Juan de Fuca Ridge, 35

Ka'imikai o Kanaloa (research vessel), 40, 41
Kerby, Terry, 41
Knorr (research vessel), 64-66

Lehman, John, 36
Loihi undersea volcano, 39-42, *43*, 44

Malahoff, Alexander, 39, 41, 42, 44
Malcom, Corey, 47-48
manganese, 36, *37*
Mariana Trench, 14
Marine (sailing vessel), 56
Mediterranean Sea, 45, 46, 48, 50, 51
Mesozoic era, 24
minerals, 35-36, *37*, 38
Mir I (research vessel), 19, 58, 69, 71
Mir II (research vessel), 19, 58, 69, 71
Momsen, Charles B., 14
"mowing the lawn," 20-21
mussels, 33, 34

Nadir (research vessel), 19, 68
National Museum of Natural History, 31
National Oceanic and Atmospheric Administration, Hawaii Undersea Research Laboratory, 39, 44
Native Americans, 10
Nautile (submersible), 18-19, 38, 68

nautilus, 18
navigation equipment, 15
Navstar (navigation satellite), 65
Nemo (submersible), 58-60
New York Zoological Society, 11
NR (Nuclear Research)-1, 50-51

Ocean Bottom Observatory, *43*

Panama Route, 55
Panic of 1857, 53
Papua New Guinea, 38
Pele's Pit, 42
Pele's Vents, 41, 42
photosynthesis, 34
Piccard, Auguste, 12-13
Piccard, Jacques, 13, 14
Pisces V (submersible), 41, 42

resins, 47
RMS Titanic Inc., 68-69
Robison, Bruce, 72
robots, 7, 9, 15, 19-21, *22*, 23
Roman wrecks, 48, 50, 51
Roper, Clyde, 31

Sansone, Frank, 41, 42, 44
satellite communications systems, 15, 65
Schatz, Barry, 54, 57
Scott, Steven D., 38
scuba, development of, 10
Sea Cliff (submersible), 18
sediment cores, 16, 17
seismometer, *40*
Shinkai 6500 (research vessel), 19
shrimp, 34
Smithsonian Institution, 31
Snoop Dog (robot), 71, 72

sonar, 15, 20, 21, 57-58
sonar sleds, 15, 19-20, 38
sonobuoys, 40
squids, 29-32, *30*
submersible, defined, 9

Thompson, Thomas G. "Tommy,"
   54, 57, 58, 60
Titanic (liner), 7-9, 19, 20, 23, 45,
   48, 58, 61, *62*, 63-69, *70*, 71-72
Titanic (movie), 63, 69, 71-72

tow fish, 20-21
transponders, 59
Trieste (bathyscaph), *13*, 13-14
tsunami, 41
tube worms, *32*, 33, 34
Tulloch, George, 69
Turtle (submersible), 18
20,000 Leagues Under the Sea
   (Verne), 30, 58

Uluburun Wreck, 45, *46*, 47

U.S. Navy, 14, 21, 50

Verne, Jules, 30, 58
Vine, Allyn C., 14
Virazon (research vessel), *48*
volcanoes, 9, 20, 39-42, 44

Walsh, Don, 14
Woods Hole Oceanographic
   Institution, Massachusetts, 7, 14,
   16, 19, 21, 45